THE ART OF
LISTENING TO
ANGELS

LILIA SHOSHANNA RAE

THE ART OF LISTENING TO ANGELS

Published by:
Transformation Books
211 Pauline Drive #513
York, PA 17402
www.TransformationBooks.com

ISBN # 978-1-945252-14-3
Library of Congress Control No: 2016957311

Cover Design: Ranilo Cabo
Layout and Typesetting: Ranilo Cabo
Editor: Marlene Oulton
Proofreader: Julie Clayton
Midwife: Carrie Jareed

Printed in the United States of America

THE ART OF
LISTENING TO
ANGELS

Acknowledgments

This book has been many years in the making. Along the way, I have not only been fully supported by angels but many friends, teachers, and family.

I would not be who I am today without the loving support of two of my closest friends, Linda Roebuck and Zemaya Jones. Zemaya made her transition to Spirit on March 1, 2016, and I miss her greatly, although she helped me finish writing from across the veil. Thankfully, Linda is still very much alive and continues to be a guiding light for me as fellow spiritual healer, teacher, author, and pilgrim to sacred sites around the world.

Over the years, I have had many teachers and mentors. I want to especially acknowledge the inspired guidance of Gloria Hesseloff, an amazing astrologer who helped me chart this path using the support of the planets and stars; Francie Boyce, a gifted energy medicine healer, who has shared her knowledge with our local community and around the globe of the impact of positive thoughts and actions on our energy; Rosemary Bredeson, "The Scientific Mystic," has helped me as coach and mentor to embody the energy of who I really am and act from that space; Mahala Connally who, as minister of my Unity church, has inspired me to practice the presence of the divine each day; Ethel Porter, who was my first Reiki teacher and who confirmed for me the many helpers in Spirit rooting for my success so that I can help them bring more light and love into the world; my friend, Margaret McHale, who introduced me to the Enneagram, a tool that was lifesaving at the time and continues to teach who I am and who I am not; Melissa Feick, who gave me my first message from the angels outside of me and continues to teach me tools to refine my intuitive gifts; Lynn Gardner, who led a group of twenty-four women on a life-changing journey to Peru in 2007; and Pat Clarke who, as one of the leaders of the Reiki community in the Annapolis, Maryland area, has supported me in my Reiki practice and spiritual teaching and healing.

As an author, I would not be where I am without Christine Kloser, the transformation catalyst, spiritual guide, and mentor. The Universe made sure that we connected through divine appointment when she put out the call for her Transformational Author Experience in 2011, and she has been a guiding light for me and so many others since then. Through her programs, I have connected with authors around the globe in *Wave One* and *Wave Five* of *Pebbles in the Pond: Transforming the World One Person at a Time.*

I want to thank the authors of all of the "Waves" for their inspiration to me and the entire planet, through their stories of transformation. I also want to thank all of Christine's staff who have helped her be the transformational leader she is and, thus, have helped me in this transformational process.

A few brave souls were willing to review my work along the way, and their feedback helped me improve the final product. Dennis and Linda Kolb read my first iteration, and even though not much of that version has survived the intervening years of editing, their support in those early years helped me to continue writing. Linda and Ed Roebuck have given me great suggestions and support many times over the years. Julie Stamper, an author in *Pebbles in the Pond, Wave Four* and who is creating an Angel House Retreat in Colorado, gave me great feedback and a beautiful visual of seeing my work on a bookshelf at her retreat. Lauren Perotti, one of my fellow authors in *Pebbles in the Pond, Wave Five*, took time while she was finishing her book to review my first chapters and suggest better ways to organize them. I thank Marlene Oulton, my editor, for her support and encouragement even before we knew she would be my editor. I also thank Julie Clayton who added her editing talents to make it a better book.

I could not leave out my appreciation and deep gratitude for the inspired leadership and teaching of James Tyberonn and the Earth-Keeper family that is part of my soul family. We have travelled to many sacred sites and explored many realms together. Each gathering and pilgrimage took me to a higher level of soulful evolution.

Lastly, but only because they rate a special mention, I want to thank my family. Most of them probably don't know what to make of me at this point in my life, but they continue to show me love beyond measure. I am truly blessed. My dad continues to inspire at age ninety-eight with his positive attitude and emphasis on eating right and being of service. My children, Mehdi, Zara, and David, support me with a love all mothers dream of. Mehdi and Zara chose spouses who show their love for me as well. My granddaughter, Baylor, shines a light so bright that I merely need to be in her presence to feel uplifted. My sisters, Charlotte and Carol, and my brother, Charlie, have always been supportive, even when having very different views on life. Their spouses, Gina, Keith, and Dan, and my nieces, Julia and Andrea, have stood by me as well. I am so grateful for all the blessings of my family. My mom, who made her transition in November 2008, made it clear through her messages, directly and through friends, that she supports and loves me. Who can ask for more?

I want to give thanks for the support that I received from countless others along the way. As the angels have reminded me, we are all one. Namaste.

Table of Contents

Introduction

For most of my life, I did not know that angels still communicated to humans. I thought they were historical creatures or perhaps reserved for those most holy. Having my heart broken three times in succession finally untethered my logical, rational mind and opened me up to a whole new understanding. Angels are alive and well. They are available to help us. We need only ask.

You may have heard this theory, and you may already speak to angels. You may have at least consulted with someone who does. On the other hand, you may feel skeptical that this is possible.

Whatever your experience with angels, I invite you to a process that welcomes angel wisdom into your life. On the one hand, it will feel glorious and magnificent. On the other, it will challenge you at the core of your being. In the art of listening to angels, you will have to listen to your soul and distinguish between the truth talk of angels and Spirit and the wily workings of your ego. That may seem like an easy task. I hope it is for you. It has not been for me. Since I don't think I am alone in this, I am sharing what I have learned so that the journey can be easier for you.

If you have doubts about receiving personal messages from angels, I want you to develop a sense of confidence to trust the experience. As you do so, your life will be enhanced. I want you to know that you are loved and know more fully the love that you are. Angels can help with that. It seems to be one of their most important jobs.

I do not consider myself an angel expert or even an expert on listening to angels. I wrote this book because I resisted their messages and guidance for years. I did not feel worthy or capable. I was scared to share my experiences, because I might be judged crazy or delusional. I let my fears of how I might be perceived by others stand in my way. I no longer want that for myself or for you.

Angels are here to help us. Why not open up and allow them to do so? Why block their wisdom and love? Isn't that what this world needs more than anything?

When I teach spiritual practices, I remind my students (and myself) to start in the present moment. Each moment contains the infinite. Being present in this moment, we open ourselves to the ocean of possibilities. This is easier said than done. Breath work helps us to become present, yet it still is not easy. We can get to that place briefly, and then a thought intervenes and we are back in the past or future. Even the focus on the breath takes us away from the present. It helps us get there, but being present requires letting go of even that awareness.

Whatever your relationship with angels, it begins with being present in the now. In this book, I break down the process of developing your relationship with angels into five simple steps:

1. Ask
2. Open your heart
3. Listen
4. Thank them
5. Act

These are simple steps, but not necessarily easy ones. Rest assured, I provide suggestions for how to remove any blocks that may appear, particularly in the listening part.

Although the process may not be easy, it is so beneficial. It can be deeply transformative. It requires being honest with yourself. It requires dropping your protective shell that you use to prevent others from seeing your truth. This type of protective device is not effective with angels because our angelic helpers can see right through it.

Whether our ego inflates our self-worth or deflates it, angels see the truth. They help us see it too, if we are willing.

That willing part is one of the coolest things about angels. They respect free will. They will not force us to do anything; they merely give us suggestions. We get to decide whether we act on them. They do not save us from the consequences of our choices, although they are always available to help us should we reconsider and follow their guidance. They are there for us with love and without judgment.

The angels told me that they need us to be messengers for them. When I heard this I wondered, *Why do angels need messengers? They are messengers themselves.* The answer was that few people are listening to them. They need messengers like us to get people to open up and hear them. How else will there be a lasting shift on this planet?

How many of you have heard their call but dismissed them as not being real or did not feel worthy of their attention? Have you been afraid of ridicule or rejection by family and colleagues for this belief? There are many excuses for blocking angels out of our lives, yet they truly want to help us, and humanity needs their help. The whole planet needs us to listen to them because of what we are doing to the earth and all life on it.

I accept the call to be a messenger for the angelic realm. I dedicate my life to being a clear vessel for angelic wisdom. It is time to open up and allow their love and light to transform our lives. Their mission is not just to give us information; it is to help us transform at our depths, for we cannot listen to them unless we are willing to change at the deepest levels—otherwise, their messages will simply bounce off the protective shells of materiality in which we have encased ourselves.

In 2016, millions around the globe watched two eaglets hatch in the US National Arboretum in Washington, DC. Video cameras were set up, and the images were streamed on the Internet. The mother sat on the eggs until the eaglets were developed enough to break through the shell. One broke open first. Viewers could see the shell crack, line by crooked line. It took a while for the eaglet to use its beak to open the shell and break free. The mother did not help, other than to try to keep it warm. Once free, the mother started feeding it with bits of food and waited for the next one to hatch. The second eaglet went through that same process of slowly cracking its shell and breaking free. Each had their own timing of entering this world, and the mother waited patiently while protecting and keeping them warm. We have to break through our shells, just like the eaglets. Our angels are ready and waiting to keep us protected and cared for, but they know that the final job is ours alone. We each have our own timing. If we are aware of our shell, it may be time to break it open.

One of our wisest scientists, Albert Einstein, said that a problem cannot be solved using the same thinking with which it was created. We have spent centuries trying to solve 3-D problems using 3-D solutions. Why do we not listen to the scientific wisdom we have been given and look for solutions from higher dimensions? The angels can help us do that, because they exist on those higher dimensions and have a greater perspective on the answers.

Before we can do this on a collective level, we need to do it on an individual level. We need to open up to the angelic wisdom that is available to us. As we do this, we will impact those around us—our families, friends, communities, and regions. The local impact will become global. The ripples of love and light that we open to from the angelic realm will spread around the planet.

Are you ready? Are you willing to open up to the love and light that is divinely provided by angels who are ready to assist? Are you willing to explore how this might be possible for you?

Let us begin in the present moment. It begins with asking. Please join me as I tell my story and share how you too can develop the art of listening to angels.

PART I

LISTENING TO ANGELS

CHAPTER 1

How It Began for Me

During the tenth year of my marriage, my life crumbled. I had two wonderful children, and the third had not yet been conceived. I felt like I was in hell and had no way out. The man who had said he loved me enough to commit to a lifetime together changed into a man I feared would kill me. He was consumed with a paranoid jealousy that I could not dissuade or console. I did not know what to do. I was afraid to tell anyone, because I thought that would incite a rage he could not stop. I prayed. I cowered in a corner of our dining room, because he could come at me from only one direction that way. I am not sure what good that would have done, but I was desperate for some sense of protection.

This went on for six months. Each day, there were moments when he was the sweet, loving man I had married. He held and caressed me. I thought, *My prayers have been answered. He has found his way back to sanity and the love we share.* Then abruptly, his voice would change, and he became the prosecutor, interrogating me about where I had been, who I had talked to, and why I took so long to get home. He asked the same questions repeatedly and made me swear that I was telling the truth. I kept trying to reassure him I was not lying and had not betrayed our vows.

In the making up and beginning again, my third child was conceived, but the cycles of abuse continued. One morning, the threats escalated a notch. I realized that as scary as it was to run away and risk being found by him, staying was not an option. I had to leave him and take my children with me.

I called my mom. My parents had no idea what I had been experiencing because I had told them nothing. My husband was a loving, light-hearted man to everyone but me, and I had been too scared to let anyone know differently. My mom jumped into protector mode. She called Dad, and he arranged for us to say in a hotel that was near the National Security Agency. It is no longer there, but at that time it provided me with a sense of security. Little did I know that I had even more protection working for me on the other side of the veil.

Once I divorced, he left the area and never contacted me or my children again. As hard as that has been for them, I know that if he had stayed, we never would have enjoyed the peace his leaving allowed. He had many good traits—which is why I had first fallen in love with him. Yet his behavior toward the end of our marriage prevented me from feeling safe or trusting that he would not harm me.

I was not ready to give up on finding love in my life, though. A few years after my divorce, I met someone and fell in love. I spent five years with him, thinking he would come to love me as much as I loved him. I was rudely awakened when he left me for someone else.

Within a few months of that breakup, I met another great love who I was sure was "the one." We were soul mates! I could feel it. I came to learn that despite our soul connection, he chose my best friend instead. There I was, broken wide open by the second of two significant heartbreaks in one year, while still healing from my excruciating divorce. It was devastating. I felt betrayed by my friend and crushed by the rejection of my soul mate! I felt unlovable.

Angels Came to the Rescue

At the time of the last heartbreak, I was working full-time as a government lawyer and raising three children on my own. Despite my grief, I had to keep going, if only for their sake. During my lunch breaks I took walks to clear my head and make sense of what felt like a gaping hole in my heart. On one of these walks I had a strange conversation in my mind. I visualized a small being sitting on my left shoulder, dressed in a black suit and fedora. This character told me about love and the need to love myself, reassuring me that I was lovable. I asked him who he was. He said, "Harry. I am your guardian angel." You can imagine how odd that seemed. I was a lawyer!

Despite my confusion, I allowed the conversation to continue. It felt comforting to talk to someone about how devastated and alone I felt. He told me I was lovable even if I didn't feel this way. He reassured me that the hole in my heart would heal.

As I listened to him, a part of me wondered if I had lost my marbles along with my heart. The experience felt real, so I continued to have conversations with him. After a few more lunchtimes talking with Harry, I felt a second presence, an energy hovering over my right shoulder. I did not have a visual other than a cloud-like form of energy. Figuring that I was already a bit nuts, I began talking to this field of energy. Again I was reassured that I was loved and lovable. I asked this energy if it had a name. He said it was Michael. *Could this be Archangel Michael?* I did not have the courage to ask him. I thought that archangels talked only to special people like Mother Mary or Joan of Arc. It was bad enough that I had an ordinary angel talking to me. I was not going to suggest this was an archangel, so I let him be plain Michael for a while.

These lunchtime encounters with Harry and Michael continued for a few weeks until I had to find out if I was going over the edge. I did not want to talk to anyone about these conversations, but I remembered that there was a bookstore close to where I walked every day at lunch. I thought there might be a book that could help me figure out what was going on. I walked down several aisles in the bookstore and to a section that had religious materials. I saw a section marked "Angels." I pulled out a few books, but nothing struck me as helpful. I started to leave when I heard Michael say, "Look more closely. There is a book there that will help." I went back and looked more closely at each book in that section. One jumped out: *Angelspeake: How to Talk with Your Angels.*[1] That sounded appropriate. It was written by two sisters, Barbara Mark and Trudy Griswold, who spoke with angels and helped others learn how to do this. I bought it and devoured it in one sitting.

The authors told of their experiences communicating with the angelic realm and leading workshops to help others open up to messages from angels. They suggested the simple act of taking a pen in hand and asking for a message. When I finished the book that night, I sat at my computer and began typing my conversations with Harry and Michael.

As blessed as these early messages were, my life continued much as it had before. I felt like I was living in two worlds. In one world, I connected with the Divine and had mystical experiences. I communicated with angels and explored the unknown. In my other world, I was a mother raising three children on her own, spending a lot of time watching them play sports, and talking to other parents about our children's latest fashion craze or what was happening in school. In that world, I was a lawyer supervising other lawyers in a government office—not an environment for talking about my most recent communiques from Archangel Michael.

I wanted to leave my job and explore this new world that I found so intriguing and affirming. I wanted to read, write, meditate, go to spiritual workshops, and forget about the mundane plane where I had to use my left-brain and be practical. It was hard to feel so exhilarated by what came streaming into my morning meditation and then have to snap back into ordinary reality, making sure my kids ate breakfast and had their lunch money and homework assignments before they rushed out the door to catch the bus.

I could not tell my children or the rest of my family what was going on. I knew they would be concerned about my mental welfare if I told them I was communicating with Archangel Michael. Who was going to believe that? I did not want to endure the skepticism, so I kept my experiences to myself. It was better to live in a divided world in which I felt safe to explore my new discoveries than to come out of my closet and risk rejection or scorn from my family, neighbors, and colleagues.

Before my angel experiences, I had no real sense of purpose other than to do what was necessary to take care of my children. My focus was more on daily life than anything else. After my initial awakening, I realized that my heart was yearning to go in a different direction—still handling the third-dimensional responsibilities but moving with a sense of a higher purpose. I began contemplating what I came here to do in this life. Birthing and raising my three beautiful children was a big piece of my purpose, yet my heart was telling me there was more for me to do. I still longed for a relationship, but in retrospect I was longing for a love that was beyond the human variety, and a sense of purpose in bringing more love into the world.

Additional Resources Helped

When I started my communication with Harry, I had no idea that I was shifting into a new plane of understanding about life in the spiritual realm or, for that matter, life itself. As I understood the spiritual realm more fully, I saw that the only separation from it is within our perception and thoughts.

There is so much assistance in the angelic realm. Turn to any book on angels and you will be amazed at how many have been named, each with a different gift and purpose. Soon after my encounters with Harry and Archangel Michael, I read more books, because I did not know anyone else who communicated with angels. One of the more influential books, *The Messengers*,[2] recounts how angels started communicating with Nick Bunick. He began encountering the number 444 in all sorts of mysterious ways, and he realized that it connected him to angels. After reading the book, I started seeing the number 444 on my digital clock, on store receipts, and in other places. It was evidence to me that angels want to communicate with us, and the number 444 is one signal to let us know they are available.

Another book with special meaning was *Inspired by Angels,* by Sinda Jordan.[3] It shared messages from four archangels: Michael, Raphael, Gabriel, and Uriel. I kept the book by my meditation spot and turned to it when I wanted inspiration. I found that I could open it to whatever page felt right, and a message with particular significance for me would be there. By reading these messages, I received wise guidance and developed a personal connection to each of these archangels.

Another great resource for me is a deck of cards called *Angel Blessings.*[4] Kimberly Marooney designed the cards with artistic renditions of forty-four angels. Her process is an inspiration in itself. While recovering from a serious illness, she was visited by angels who inspired her to create the cards so that others could communicate with the angelic realm. She was shown the vision, and she followed through. She used her inner guidance rather than more traditional descriptions and hierarchies, so some of the descriptions vary from other sources, but angels are not one-dimensional beings. They have many gifts. What matters most is the personal relationship that someone develops with a particular angel.

I am guided to choose a card from the deck as I am writing, with the intention of receiving a message appropriate for this book. As with any card deck that I use for divining spiritual messages, I turn my attention inside, align myself with my Higher Self, and ground that energy by connecting to the earth so that inspiration of the highest caliber can come through. I hold the cards in my hands and state the intention. I pick whatever card feels right, and it is amazing how this process brings a message of great inspiration that feels perfect for the moment.

Doing this now, I felt a call from all of the cards. It was almost as if their angelic counterparts were saying, "Pick me! Pick me! I want to help. I am here. Me too. Me too." It took me longer than usual to select the card that felt right. I stopped a few times but kept mixing them up. One card suddenly flew out of the deck. I am blown away by what just happened. Although I have done this kind of thing for many years, there is always that niggling doubt about whether the "perfect" card will show up or if it is my imagination, a story I tell myself. Guess which angel showed up? Michael. I don't have a witness here to vouch for me, but I have no reason to make this up.

I take a moment to appreciate and give thanks for what just happened. This is Spirit working in real time, and this is how it has been whenever I have worked on writing this book. When I take the time to turn inward and connect to Spirit in the way I just described for picking a card, Spirit shows up in a way I cannot deny. In this case, Michael let me know that he supports me in this writing, in this moment, just as he has from the start.

Thank you, Michael. Do you have a message that you want to come through me in this moment?

Yes, Lilia. I want you to know that I am very much present and available to you as you write and as you grow in your spiritual awareness. You have grown tremendously over the years of your spiritual awakening, and yet you still doubt your ability to communicate with me in a way that is authentic, clear, and truthful. Please take this as a sign that the connection is strong and true. It is not your imagination. It is important to share your experience with others so they can know that we are available to help. We need only for the person to open up their awareness to the possibility and allow the communication to come through. It is as easy and as difficult as that. Getting ego-based doubts out of the way is the hardest part.

We love you and love what you are doing, and yes, the other angels would love to communicate with you.

Michael, I am so grateful for the way you have shown up in my life so powerfully and in this moment. It reaffirms my belief that I am writing for a reason: to help others have these types of experiences and be enriched by the love and wisdom that is available. We need only ask! How many times have I heard and written that down? This is one more confirmation, and a powerful one at that, because I did not expect it. I knew there would be a great message from whatever angel card I selected, but your card jumped out of the deck so that I could not miss it. I am still blown away with emotion. Thank you. Thank you. Thank you.

I would like to turn to Kimberly Marooney's description that accompanies this card to see if there is another inspirational message. The first paragraph is perfect.

"Archangel Michael is dedicated to the preservation of the spiritual destiny of every soul. He loves you with an intensity you cannot yet imagine as he patiently watches you, life after life, fanning the flickering embers of your soul fire on the altar of your heart, until the flame of enthusiasm and love of God burn brightly enough to consume your limitations and set you free!"[5]

How beautiful. What a wonderful image of the love of God burning away any limitations that we may feel and set us free. Michael is available to remind us of that powerful love.

What Are the Signs, and How Do We Recognize Them?

How do we know if we are communicating with angels? We each get different signals to let us know that an angel wants to speak to us or give us a message. I feel an energy, and hear words that I do not identify as mine. This is often followed by chills running down my arms or spine. Feeling chills through some part of your body is such a common phenomenon, and I often hear people say something like, "I felt my hair standing on end." This is often discounted as something we are making up or making too much of, but we do ourselves a disservice if we do not recognize it. Angels are letting us know that they are present and want to communicate.

Some people have more visual clues, as shown in my experience during a massage session with a friend. Before beginning, she checked my *chakras* (energy points in the subtle body) and saw that they were closed down. When she asked what I was afraid of, I realized that I had been absorbed by the fear of moving on in my life. Even though I was not aware of the effects on my body, it was clear that my fear was shutting down my chakras and affecting my body's flow of energy.

As my friend worked on my chakras and had me work on releasing my fears, I had an understanding that if I can "know" in my body that all is in divine order, then everything I need is provided for and will be provided for; I have nothing to fear. I had a real sense in mind and body what that "knowing" was about.

As that understanding settled into my body, my friend said she felt a wave of energy go through her body, and she saw blue lights. I asked her what that meant to her. She said that it indicated Michael's presence and that she worked with Michael often. I realized that the information about "knowing" was coming to me from Michael.

More recently, Michael used color to announce his presence through someone else. I took a workshop on the use of color for healing and spiritual development. As I worked on the exercises, aqua spoke to me as a color to work with for developing my healing practice and attracting clients. During a coaching session with the workshop leader, she said she saw Michael bringing an aqua color into our session. That brought great joy to me, because I had not associated that shade of blue with him before. It was clear he was letting me know that he was working with me even when I was not aware of it. Having that awareness, I felt even stronger about following my calling and doing what I came into this body to do. Part of this calling is to let others know of the assistance we have in the spiritual realm. They want to help us.

Whether the signs are visual, auditory, or sensory, or if they happen through synchronicities that have too great a meaning to be random, angels will do what they can to get our attention. I was a tough case. I needed to be totally broken open by a series of heartbreaks. Even after I started the process, I allowed doubts, unworthiness, and other blocks to prevent me from having a consistent and open communication. Through seeing how difficult it can be and how important this work is, I share my experiences so others can allow angels to come in to their life. If I can do it, so can you.

CHAPTER 2

Why Learn this Art?

My experiences with angels may sound interesting to you—hearing voices, feeling energy, and seeing colors—but what is the point in developing this skill? It can get tricky, because our ego plays games with us. Not all voices in our heads are angels. Some were planted in our neural pathways long ago, playing familiar old tunes that have kept us stuck in ruts. The familiar refrains are "You are not good enough... Play it safe or you will get hurt...Who do you think you are?... You are getting too big for your britches!" Even when we hear something new, we can wonder if we are hearing it correctly or identifying its source accurately.

Figuring out which messages are conditioned responses, latent fears, or truly crazy ideas is not easy. There is a trust factor to be developed: trust in your ability to discern what is true for you. That can be difficult if you do not have a lot of trust in yourself. Developing that trust is an art. Skilled painters begin with a crayon or pencil before they move on to using brushes and mixing paint on a palette. Taking small steps in this art of listening to angels will help you trust in yourself. They love to help, so ask them to assist you in the process.

Angels Are Here to Help Us

One reason to develop the art of listening to angels is because they exist to help us. I don't know why they were created that way. I do know that they are part of the divine design, as immense and incomprehensible as that is. The "why" does not matter so much, because as we open up to their assistance, we see how much they want to help and the amazing number of ways they do. I have been working with them for years and keep opening up further to their wisdom and assistance. I know they would love for me to consult with them more often, but I have had to remove my personal blocks along the way. As I develop more trust in myself as a messenger, a clear channel, and an accurate receiver, I open up to more important, more detailed messages. I am still learning how to do this effectively. It takes work on myself to do this well.

One instance showed me how much more I had to learn. My coach and mentor, who is an extremely clear channel for messages from the Spirit realm, told me during a session that the angels wanted to work with me on some classes I was developing. I balked. I told her, "I don't know whether I will hear them well enough." I did not have enough trust in myself. I knew that they would give me exactly what I needed, but my lack of trust that I was hearing correctly held me back. The self-esteem thing was part of my personal growth work. As I chip away at that issue and others, the communications come through much more clearly and precisely.

Another clairvoyant mentor told me that I resisted my gift because I allowed the other "voices" to muddle the messages. I had not realized that it was critical to quiet those other "voices" (the conditioned ones that I had not let go of) to hear the angelic ones without interruption or distortion. Once I recognized this, I was able to communicate much more easily.

A third messenger for the angels told me that I needed to clear the physical clutter in my surroundings so that it did not distort the clarity of the messages. I acted on this and found that it was much easier to tune in and hear them. I also enjoyed being in my home much more once my surroundings were more peaceful.

When I set my intention to communicate, I hear an answer or feel a loving presence. I don't need to know why the angels are available. I just need to recognize that they *are* available and be willing to work with them for my highest good and for the highest good of all who I impact, whether in service or relationship. As I am helped by the angels, I am able to help others. It is a beautiful, expansive process that keeps on giving.

Angels Know Things We Don't

Angels respect our free will. That is why we start by asking them for help. Some angelic interventions require no conscious request for help, but this is explained by an agreement before the individual's life began or as a request from the soul when the conscious self was not able to ask.

Angels are not restricted by time and space limitations. I do not fully understand this concept, but I know that being free of these limitations, they can know much that we do not. We *can* understand that what they share with us is for our highest good. That is part of how they were created.

Not giving me information can also be for my highest good. I can ask for the winning numbers of the Mega Millions lottery, but it may not be in my best interest to win. It seems an irreverent way to use a sacred gift. I have asked for help in finding parking spaces, and that has worked many times. Some might say that too is a sacrilegious use of angelic assistance. My sense is that they are willing to help us with mundane issues as long as the assistance moves us in the direction of our highest good.

One of the more mundane but important messages I have received from my angels was when I lost my government identification card. It was going to cost fifty dollars to replace, and if I lost the replacement, it would cost another hundred, so I was anxious about finding it. I had looked everywhere, including inside my car. I was about to lock the door and go back into my house when I heard, "Open the passenger door and look there." When I did, I saw that the card had slipped into the pocket of that door and was hard to see from the driver's side. I was grateful and expressed my appreciation many times. Angels may withhold information too, if we are not ready to receive it. If we knew in advance all of the changes we would make by following their advice, we might cling to the old path like a lifeline.

When I started writing this book I thought it would be easy. I would write about my experiences with Harry and Michael, and it would be as easy as the conversations I had with them. Little did I know that the writing would lead me on an eight-year journey of self-excavation and deep purging of fears. I had no idea how many layers of doubt I would have to clear. If I had known this at the beginning I would have said, "Let someone else go down that road. The terrain is too rough for me." When working with angels, discerning what type of assistance is appropriate is a personal thing. It is between you and the angels working with you. You will get a sense of incorrectness if something is not appropriate. They are not meant to live your life for you. That is your job. They are assistants in that process.

What about asking angels to help us in our work, such as planning a class as my coach suggested? When I do this, I find that I receive ideas and inspiration that makes the class better than I could design on my own. I also receive ideas that are specific to a student in the class. For example, I was going to lead a meditation class one day and I asked for help with one aspect of the class. I felt guided by my angels to lead one of the practice meditations in a specific way and found that one student needed it done exactly as my guide had suggested. I could not have known that on my own. By asking angels for help, they could check on what was best for each student and guide me in that direction. I had to be open to the guidance. I may not have known how best to design this aspect if I had not asked, listened, and acted on it.

Some may wonder how this is different from intuition. It works in the same way. It is not necessary to identify a particular angel or even to identify it as angelic communication. Tuning in to what feels true is what is important. When I identify a message as angelic, it feels more complete. Yet, discerning what feels true rather than identifying the source is more important.

Angels can help with a range of issues. During a session I had with a friend, the angels competed for a chance to speak. It was humorous. It reminded me of the time that I chose a card from the *Angel Blessings* deck while I was writing the first chapter of this book. It was as if the angels were again saying, "Pick me! Pick me!" Angels can be funny. They do not always have to be serious, and neither do you as you work with them.

The first angel who spoke during my session with my friend identified itself as a money angel. I liked that it had a generic name rather than a traditional name with a less obvious gift and purpose. The money angel gave me great insights on how to get into the flow of my life and allow it to happen. The angel advised me that as I open to the divine flow of being on purpose, resources will flow to me, and resistance to the flow will block the resources.

Next was a healing angel. This one told me that the key to healing was for the healer to get in touch with the healing place inside of them. The healing angel said that we each have that special place inside us through which we get in touch with wholeness and all of the attributes of wholeness: peace, love, joy, serenity, truth, and abundance. From there, we can help others get in touch with the healing place inside them.

The angel emphasized that healers do not "heal." Each individual heals their body as they get into that healing place inside. This advice conformed to my understanding of the healing process. It also served as a timely reminder. It came as one of my closest friends, Zemaya, was approaching her time of transition. Although I was not able to help her stay in physical form, the angels assured me that she did what she needed to do before she made her transition. They helped me see that it was not up to me to find a "cure" so that she could live. As hard as it was to lose her, they let me know that it was her time to move to the Spirit realm.

After the healing angel spoke, I asked whether the angels had anything to say about my writing. They said that the answer was to write the book. They were eager to work with me if I would only listen! They said I needed only to take dictation. I did my best to get out of the way and be a clear channel for them in the words you see on these pages.

I would also like to share another experience with an angel while working with one of my mentors. She is a gifted intuitive, certified angel therapy practitioner, and teacher of many other esoteric and healing practices. As part of a class on developing intuitive skills, she often introduced the students to an ascended master or archangel before focusing on a method for using our power of intuition. On one occasion, she introduced us to Archangel Raziel. I had never worked with Raziel before. By directing us to go into a meditative state and mentioning his name, we were able to feel his energy, have visual images, and communicate with him.

It is hard to explain this feeling, and everyone will have a different experience when communicating with the Spirit realm. For me, each "entity" (for lack of a better word) has a different feel. Although each entity may appear differently to different people, there are usually some distinguishing characteristics.

My experience of Raziel was that he was more angular. His form seemed defined by lines set at particular angles instead of the typical angelic form, which is more curvaceous, a human-like form with wings. His energy still felt loving and nurturing. I found it curious that I experienced his energy that way, as I had never visualized angelic energy in that manner before. The teacher shared that one of Raziel's gifts is to help us work with sacred geometry, which is all about angles and lines that connect to circles and spheres and flow into life-giving energy. The angular lines that I felt in his energy field made sense as a visual construct to connect him with this aspect of sacred geometry.

The word Kimberly Marooney associates with Raziel is "knowledge." Part of the message she says Raziel brings to us is this:

"Raziel is deeply involved with us, bringing the knowledge we seek when we encounter certain mysteries on our spiritual path. These mysteries range from finding the cause of a personal illness or self-destructive behavior to having the desire to access and understand universal truths."[6]

How wonderful to know that these beings in the Spirit realm have such wonderful gifts. The possibilities are endless if we allow ourselves to believe and act on our beliefs. Imagine the blessings we can bring into our lives and those of others.

Each time I read about one of the angels in Kimberly's book, *Angel Blessings,* or the many books on angels, I remember how much there is to life beyond what we experience in our daily routine. When we take the time to get to know even one of the beings from the angelic realm, we expand our awareness and uplift our consciousness. Because they exist in such a high vibration of love, opening up to their gifts can only raise our own vibration.

Angels Know Us Better Than We Know Ourselves

Because angels live in the Spirit realm, which allows them to see so more than we can in this denser plane, they have access to information that we do not have, unless we have developed the skills of shamans and yogi masters to access information available on other planes. I have not fully developed those skills, but I am learning and have met many modern mystics who have developed them. In the meantime, I appreciate being able to ask angels to help me understand what I need to know to improve my life.

When I ask for assistance, I often hear, *You are on the right track. You also may want to....* The angels provide suggestions. If I feel sad or disappointed, I am consoled by words like, *You are loved, you are lovable, you are love.* These messages are usually followed by a specific suggestion on what to do or how to look at what happened differently. I know I get what I need. My mood shifts, and I see how to proceed in a way that serves me better than venturing on my own.

Listening to the guidance received and acting on it can be hard because we rarely have all of the information that the angels do. I was led to retire from my job in July 2010. It was an early retirement and I took a financial penalty, but I knew that I wanted to move toward my purpose and was struggling to do that while working full time. Although I enjoyed my work, I felt called to do something more spiritual.

A few months after retiring, I was given the opportunity to go on a two-week trip to Bolivia with a group of "light workers," a term I use for those who have a passion or purpose to bring more light and love into the world. I had met many of the group through my involvement with the organization sponsoring the trip. The trip was originally planned for December but then was moved to February. I would not have been able to go on that trip if I had been working full time, because my job prohibited leave time from January to mid-April. Even though I went back to work contractually that winter, I was able to include a clause in the contract for time off for that two-week period. The trip was a unique event that could not have taken place any other time. I had experiences that could have happened only with that group of people in that place. I know the angels knew that I had to be free to go on it. They worked with me to take that leap into retirement even when I knew it was not financially feasible. Later, I returned to work on a part-time basis because I did not have the rest of the financial picture figured out, but by listening to their guidance, I was able to go on that life-changing trip.

I sometimes joke that it was an awfully expensive trip because of the reduced retirement allocation I chose to receive, but I would not trade my experiences on that trip for any amount of money. The angels knew how important the trip would be. I thought I was retiring to write a book and start a healing and teaching practice. It was not yet time for that, but it was time to prepare in a way that I could not have done if I were still working full time.

One area in which I still struggle is intimate relationships. I have had my share of loving ones, but the one that I consider "ideal" has eluded me. As I shared in the first chapter, it was a failed marriage and a series of significant heartbreaks that opened me up to hearing angels. Consequently, much of my early communication focused on my love life, or what was more of a "not feeling loved" life. They kept reassuring me that I was both loved and lovable. They added, *You are love.* I needed to hear that over and over. I did not understand what they were saying until I stopped seeking love outside of me. *I am* love. We are all love. We keep forgetting that and seek it outside ourselves.

I believe one of the key reasons angels are working with us is to remind us that we are love in action. Love births through us. When we look to others or to situations or substances for the love we seek, we can't help but be disappointed. It is not there. Love is who we are and why we came into this life. Why is it so hard for us to see? It is not hard for angels to see, and they remind us daily if we let them.

Working with angels has an interesting side benefit. We get to work on ourselves as we work on developing the communication with them. The steps in the process help us to do the work we need to make the message system work. Angels help us along the way if we feel stuck. That is the beauty of working with them. It is also the challenge, because if the communication is not happening in the way we want, it is ourselves that we have to deal with, not them. That can be daunting. They require us to face the truth about ourselves, and that can be scary. They are loving and compassionate, forgiving, patient, kind, and resourceful. They embody the good qualities we aspire to, and they can help us overcome whatever is in our way.

I had to own up to my issues of self-worth, bad habits, lack of discipline, and other issues that I hated. I recognize them as blocks to hearing the beautiful guidance that is readily available. These blocks prevent me from moving forward on my path of evolution and my path of service. That being said, in the act of acknowledging them, I have a choice. Do I do something about it, or do I remain blocked? Working with angels helps me do something, even if it is taking baby steps. Working with angels requires me to be truthful with myself. They are truthful to me in the kindest, most loving way, and they do not allow me to lie to myself. That can be both a gift and a challenge. Living life truthfully is not easy, but why live any other way? For ease in the moment? For a false sense of comfort? Do you want to reach the end of your life and look back at missed opportunities?

This is an ongoing process. Thankfully, in each moment we can choose again. I am grateful that I have assistance along the way. Even when I ignore that assistance and live unconsciously through habit, seeking comfort instead of truth, tolerating what I don't like instead of liberating what I hope for, they are there for me. Even when I lose patience, erupt in anger, retreat in fear, or lie to myself, they are there for me. They are there with love, joy, peace, wisdom, understanding, solutions, and more. All I have to do is ask.

CHAPTER 3

The AOLTA
(The Art of Listening to Angels)

Y ou would think that given all of these wonderful experiences with Archangel Michael and others that I would have it made. All we need to do is ask, right? They are always available to us, correct? Although grateful for my blessings, I am also keenly aware of the unresolved challenges in my life. What has been in my way? What do I now know about how to remove blocks? Removing blocks and opening up to the beautiful messages of Spirit is what the art of listening to my angels is all about.

I can hear a thousand times from Michael that I am loved, lovable, and loving, and it feels good each time. Then life turns upside down, I land on the ground with a loud thump, and I see the props and scenery of my old 3-D world and wonder what happened. I spend weeks or months wandering around, forgetting that I felt differently and that there is another way to live. Eventually, I remember to call on Michael. I ask what happened, and he tells me that I simply forgot.

This is about figuring out how to be the spiritual being I am in this human body. I can learn how to do this from angels, saints, sages, and even the voice of God, but understanding what to do with the messages is the art of soul-filled living. Gurus and sages, mystics and masters have advised us through the ages. We have sacred texts that describe the process in detail. The Vedas and the Upanishads are the oldest of these texts—we also have sacred texts of Judaism, Christianity, and Islam. When are we going to wake up to what life on this planet is about?

The angels ask me to listen. They tell me that I am blocking their messages by the chatter in my mind. They tell me that my sense of unworthiness won't let truth stay in my body and that my fears are guiding me, not my soul.

The Art of Listening to Angels (AOLTA) as told to me by the angels, is a five-step process. This also stands for Ask, Open your heart, Listen, Thank them, and Act. Each step is broken down into sub-steps, because as simple as they are, there is more involved in making them work. I am grateful to my angels for this process.

Step 1: Ask for Assistance

Asking Requires Awareness

A crucial step in communicating with angels is asking for their help. They respect free will, so asking signals that it is our will that they help. This step requires an awareness of what is possible. Before my initial encounters, I did not know that it was possible for someone like me to have that kind of interaction. I was not aware of anyone else around me having such experiences.

Until midlife, I attended a traditional Protestant church that did not talk of angels except in connection with Christmas stories or as the subject of a sermon or Sunday School lesson. Even my Aunt Mabel, who was instrumental in my early spiritual education and devoutly read the Bible before dawn each morning, did not talk of angelic interactions except in a biblical context. Her focus was on Jesus as her lord and savior. She prayed to him, and I imagine she heard guidance from him, but she kept quiet on those details.

My friends who grew up as Catholics told me that angel awareness was more a part of their curriculum. If they went to Catholic school, they were told that each child had a guardian angel. They learned about Catholic saints who had encounters with angels.

If I had posed the question for myself, I could have found that books on angels were widely available in bookstores and libraries (which I discovered once I had my own angelic interaction). I lived life based on faulty assumptions until my series of heartbreaks opened me to hear Harry and Michael.

Because you are reading this book, you must have an awareness that angels exist today just as they always have. Although it is not necessary to understand the traditional angel hierarchies, it is helpful to know that the types of angels are diverse. Each has a specific role, in much the same way that each human has a unique purpose. Sometimes I ask a specific angel to help me. As an alternative, and to expand my awareness of the diversity among angels, I let my angel cards direct me to the appropriate one for the moment. At other times I ask generically, "Angels, help me with this." I like to keep life as simple as possible. The last thing the angels want is for us to be blocked because we are not sure which one we are talking to or whether our question is within their realm of expertise. Address them collectively if you are not sure which one to call on. You can ask for a name, but don't add stress to your process if you are not sure that you are hearing correctly. If a name is important, they will make sure you hear it. Most of the time it is irrelevant.

Set an Intention

Once you are aware that communicating with angels is possible, make a conscious choice to do so. Although Harry and Michael began talking to me before I had a full understanding of these possibilities, I had to consciously choose to continue the conversation and to learn more about it. Each time I initiate an encounter, I am consciously choosing to continue the communication.

A specific intention helps to guide the communication. Angels are meant to help us, not live our lives for us. Setting an explicit intention helps you see more clearly what you want to create or accomplish. This allows the angelic helper to give the assistance with a clear focus. This is similar to setting an intention for any spiritual practice. It is a crucial step.

Muddled questions lead to muddled answers. Asking with a clearly stated intent brings focus for you and the listener. This can be part of your meditation. As you quiet your thoughts, focus on your breath and bring to mind what you want help with. Start the conversation as you would when speaking with a friend. Give the background as you perceive it, and describe where you want help. The more natural and conversational you can be, the more comfortable it will feel. At first, conversing with no one else in the room will feel strange. Make sure you are in a private, secure space so that you don't have to explain your actions.

The intention can be for anything: global or local, profound or mundane. The angels do not care. Whatever we want help with is how they can serve. The intention can be huge as in asking for understanding when violence is erupting in some part of the world. One of my most important communications with Michael was around the terrorist attacks of September 11, using hijacked airplanes as weapons. I knew the horrific events had the potential to incite more rage. Michael reassured me and helped me focus on peace and love instead of the anger and hatred I was hearing from others. First I asked him for help. His response below is in italics.

Michael, I would like to ask your help and for the help of all angels and archangels, masters, sages, and saints, and all others who are on the Spirit side who can help us at this time. There is so much hate, anger, pain, grief, and despair. I know all of you are sending us as much light as we are willing to receive. What can we do to help bring more in?

Spend time in prayer and meditation with the intent of bringing in the light of love and peace. Envision that light entering the hearts of those in need of it. Witness to others the power of prayer and visioning. See the earth enveloped with light, soaking into the hearts of every man, woman, and child, healing their pain, anger, and grief. See the light showing them another way. See the light showing them that violence only begets more violence, that love is the only way. Feel Mother Mary's loving presence as she personifies love and compassion. She is speaking to those of the faiths most affected by this current conflict. Jews, Christians, and Muslims all know her to be the symbol for love and compassion, the one who brought into life the one filled with Christ light. She is now entering the hearts of all who welcome her to birth in them the Christ light.

That was reassuring to me at a time when there was so much potential for violence. We have seen much more violence and warfare since then, but I still practice what Michael suggested. It has brought peace into my surroundings, even if not worldwide. It is the only way for us to live if we want more peace in our world.

I usually focus on more everyday intentions. They are often about decisions related to work or a relationship and can be as minimal as choosing what to wear to an important meeting. Angels don't seem to care whether our intentions are global or personal. They want to help us.

Even if asking for help with a parking spot, we connect to how this will help us act in the moment. It is not as if there is a limit on how many times they can help. It is as open-ended as the boundaries of our Universe.

Ask with Humility, Vulnerability, and Honesty

To prepare for communication, we must recognize our place in the realm of creation. We are *co-creators*, and our part is vital, and yet the *co* part of the word is essential. We co-create our world in concert with the Divine and each other. The angels are in alignment with Divine will and can help guide us in that co-creative process, but we need to do our part. Three traits are vital: humility, vulnerability, and honesty. These set the stage as we start by asking for their help.

Humility

Too often, we inflate our role in the world. Sometimes this is done through ignorance, selfishness, greed, fear, or some other negative motivation. True humility knows our particular role: to understand Divine will and choose whether to align with it. If we do not take the step to determine Divine will, we are not acting with humility.

It is easy to get carried away when we first experience an angel talking to us, particularly an archangel. We can feel special and honored. The ego can have a field day if we do not understand our role in the whole process. We *are* special and honored, yet so is everyone else, whether they have an angelic visitation or not. Some may feel that they are extra special if they have a visual contact with beings from another realm. The more sensory and detailed the communication, the clearer the message can come through, but it should not be cause for an inflated ego. If you find yours flaring because of the quality of an encounter, take a moment and breathe. Allow the ego to deflate on the outbreath. Remember that the message is important, not the vessel through which it flows.

True humility does not ask us to give our power away. Low self-worth has no place here. I had to learn that lesson through many tough experiences. I compared my skills to others and felt unworthy. It does not matter if you are less experienced than someone else when speaking with angels. What matters is that you become the clearest vessel as possible. It is to claim your power and align it with the Divine. False humility keeps you from providing the service asked of you. It needs to be removed as much as the inflated ego.

True humility walks a fine line. Angels can help us know the difference. That can be part of the intention in the asking.

Vulnerability

If we have our defenses up, the messages will be cut off or distorted. It can take great personal strength to be vulnerable and present with no pretense or judgment. Be yourself. You may feel naked and unsafe, particularly if you are used to hiding behind a shell. Allow yourself to be seen. Recognize that they see you as you are. No pretenses are needed.

This may feel scary, but remember that they love you, warts and all. They do not judge you, and if you need to keep some walls up at first, they will understand. They want you to feel safe and protected. As you become more comfortable you can start removing a brick or two. You will find that doing so allows more love and light to flow from them. When you have done this, you might be willing to take a sledgehammer to your false pretenses.

Most of us learn to put up strong defenses against what could hurt. Being vulnerable may be one of the toughest steps to take in being open to angelic wisdom for someone who has strong protection mechanisms in place. If you find it difficult, let the angels know what you are feeling. They don't have to be told, but by being honest about your feelings you will find that you open up more.

Honesty

Honesty with yourself and your angels is vital. If you feel scared, admit it. If you feel better putting limitations on the experience, do that and be honest about it.

You can try to show only some of the cards in your hand, but before long, you will see that holding back does not serve you. With more practice, you will relax into the process and trust them and yourself.

When I open up to the angelic realm, I feel uplifted and expansive. I may have to face some tough truths, but as I allow them to work with me, the truths don't feel so harsh. Recently, I asked for help because my feelings got hurt. Someone I considered a friend was no longer talking to me. As I opened up to the guidance of my angels, they helped me see that I had been insensitive to her. It was tough to recognize that part of the problem was my fault. I like to think of myself as a loving, considerate person, but they showed me that I had ignored her when she needed me to reach out. They helped me see that sometimes I am so focused on what is going on in my life that I do not pay attention to those around me. It was not a judgment but an awareness. It felt uncomfortable because I wanted to hold onto my perception of being kind and considerate all the time. Having this awareness may not repair that relationship, but it will help me be the person I want to be.

I could have argued with the angels, saying, "But surely I could not be seen as unkind!" Bringing humility, vulnerability, and honesty to the process allowed me to see that from my friend's perspective, I was unkind. In the future, I can choose to be less focused on myself.

Since honesty is so vital to angel communications, consider how authentically you speak in normal conversation. Do you speak only your truth to close friends? Do you sometimes hide the truth from them? We have to be willing to be in truth as clearly as we can discern it to be in communication with the Spirit realm. Whether we are speaking to angels or others in Spirit who are in tune with our highest good (and that condition is important), being in truth is crucial. Our highest good requires it even if that level of truth is not easy to share.

One of my coaches asked me to tune into what was blocking me at the moment. The thought bubbled up that I did not feel worthy of my calling. I became nauseous at the idea that it could be something I believed. I had done so much work around self-worth that I thought I had let it go completely, but it bubbled up from my unconscious when asked the question. I could have denied its truth, but what about the nausea? What could I make of that if not a signal from my body that I could not deny? I chose to recognize the truth that even though I had done a lot of work around that issue, there were remnants in my unconscious that blocked me from accepting the worthiness of my calling. Instead of denying the belief still working me, I chose to acknowledge it and to consciously let it go.

So it is with communication with angels and others in Spirit. If we are not willing to own what is true, despite the emotions that truth brings along with it, the communication will break down. This does not have to be a harsh process, though it can bring up a range of emotions. It can lead to release from the depths, but it will feel like love is leading the way. If it does not feel loving, let it go. Truth and love go hand in hand.

Any activity that requires authenticity encourages us to grow. Authenticity means living from what we perceive as true to us. Our personal truth is as close to real truth as we can ascertain it. Truth seeking is a process, but it starts with being as truthful about ourselves as we can be. That can take some tough inner work to let go of the lies we have hidden behind, ones that have formed our identity. When we live authentically we can feel naked, because we allow ourselves to be seen without masks.

Writing required me to let go of some of the walls I hid behind for years. In preparing for publication of my story in *Pebbles in the Pond—Wave Five*, I shared with my children what I had written about the end of my marriage to their father. I was shocked by the emotions that brought up for me. When my eldest texted that the story felt heavy to him and he could not talk to me until he had processed it, a flood of emotions hit me. I went to the backyard and cried like I had not done in a long time. I started remembering the rest of the story, and it was painful to remember. The next day I shared this with a friend, and she had me go deeper with it. Part of my pain was being afraid of how my children would react, now that I was being more authentic. I had been doing my best to protect them from the pain of knowing what happened. I could no longer do that and it felt scary. I did not want to let go of the role of protector, even if it was a false role.

Communication with angels and others in the Spirit realm requires us to be as real as we can be. They lovingly accept us as we are, but for the communication to flow it is paramount that we drop pretensions or false beliefs about ourselves. It is comforting, but it can feel scary. By communicating with the Spirit world, I am learning how to embrace my fears and allow them to teach me. Fears point out danger and point us in the direction of truth. Discernment helps us discriminate between the two.

We are fooling ourselves, more than we fool anybody else, if we do not live authentically. Dishonesty with ourselves will keep us in ruts and block communication with our angels. They know what is true. They can also see when it is hard for you to accept truth. Let your false walls come down.

Step 2: Open Your Heart

Connect with the Love That is You

Communicating with angels begins in the heart, because it is all about love. Angels know a much more expansive love than most humans. For the best dialogue with them, connect to your heart first. My communication started when my heart was broken open by circumstance. I hope you find an easier way to make that connection.

You are love. If you do not experience yourself as love, take that idea into your heart and allow it to rest there. Let your heart take it in, and get to know it as an idea. As we get to know ourselves as the love we are, our vibration raises, and it becomes easier to feel the connection with angelic vibration.

Our heart has great intelligence. Allow your intelligent heart to embrace the idea that you are love. You may be surprised by what your heart lets you know. You may have to remove some blocks if areas of your heart are sealed or blocked as a form of protection, but experiment with this. Depending on how foreign this idea is to you, it may take some deliberate processing. The more you know yourself as love, the more doors to the heavenly realm of angels will open to you.

I have forewarned you that opening up to angelic wisdom will change you. Connecting to the love that is you is the start of transformation—and don't worry if this seems difficult at first. You may have deep wounds to heal before knowing the love that you are. The angels will be with you as you begin. This step is not for them. It is for you so that you can have a richer experience with them. A lack of self-love will make your energy field denser and harder to reach, but they will find a way to get through to you, just as they did when I was at low points of my life. Raising your vibration by connecting to the love that you are will make the flow of the communication easier and clearer.

Allow Yourself to Become Aware of the Love That Feels Angelic

Whatever your state of self-love, the next step is opening up to love from the angelic realm. They are messengers of the Divine. They live at a higher frequency than we do.

A meditative practice will help. Whatever form of meditation or prayer you use, quiet your thoughts and become present in your body.

I start with focusing on my breath. That change of focus from the normal habits of my mind to consciously focus on the breath allows me to let go of whatever worries or concerns are working inside me. The more time that I can spend focusing on my breath, the deeper I go into the present moment. By definition, the present moment is constantly changing. How long is a moment? It is instantaneous and infinitely small. Just as the Universe is infinitely large and beyond human comprehension, the present moment is infinitely small and beyond our ability to comprehend. Any effort to comprehend it takes us away from it.

Meditation is not about effort but about relaxing into a state of effortlessness. Because most of us did not develop this skill when we were young, it takes practice to unlearn all of the habits that get in the way. That is why focusing on the breath, and refocusing on the breath when we observe the mind playing games, helps us relax into a deeper, more present state.

If you find yourself concerned about whether you are doing it correctly, turn your attention to your breath. Use an affirmation to redirect your thoughts such as "All is in divine order," "I am love, and I am loved," or "It is okay, I am perfect as I am."

Play with each step of this process. The seemingly small change in intent from "work" to "play" will lighten up the experience. Try smiling instead of frowning when you note yourself going off course. I love to incorporate smiles into my meditative practice and encourage my meditation students to do the same. Using our smile muscles triggers a message to our brain that we are happy even when we do not think we are. It is an amazingly easy way to shift our perceptions about ourselves. The simple combination of smiling and paying attention to your breath will create shifts.

In whatever shift you have made through meditation, turn your attention to the angelic love you wish to connect to. What does it feel like? Is it not worth being present to it?

Feel Yourself Connect from the Heart to Your Angel

At whatever level you feel the love of your angel, visualize the connection from your heart to it. You do not have to know the angel by name, and you do not have to do anything. The visualization will assist you in knowing that this is possible. You may not feel ready and may have resistance. There may be unexpected emotions. Whatever happens is okay. This is a process, and like any spiritual practice, it can take time. Further reflection or stepping back may be necessary to gain your bearings so that you feel safe. Be gentle with yourself and don't judge your process. Take each step when it feels right to you. Return to an earlier step if you feel blocked. Perhaps in this moment you need to open up to the love you are before you can open up to an angel's love. That is in itself part of the process, and any judgment you hold around going back to the beginning will get in your way, so let it go. The angels have repeatedly told me I am love and I am loved. I am telling you that you are love, and you are loved. The more you open up to your love, the more you will be able to open up to their love.

Step 3: Listen to Their Guidance

The third step is to listen, and that is easier than it sounds, as it is related to the need to ask with humility, vulnerability, and honesty. If you are not able to do that, you may not be able to hear. Listening requires openness. If you have blocks, find ways to remove them by being willing and asking for human help if you are not able to clear them on our own. Once you hear what they have to say, discern if what you are hearing is truth.

Open Your Mind as Well as Your Heart

The practice requires an open mind to receive the message as clearly and untainted as possible. Meditation is helpful, as it allows me to clear out the extraneous thoughts in my mind and open myself as a clear channel. In the meditation moment I can become clear on my intention for the assistance. What do I really want? What is most important to me?

Sometimes when I ask a question, doubts appear. I question my ability to hear. What if I don't like the answer? What if it does not make sense? Will I have to share it with someone else? What if those I tell think I am making it up? All of these questions are thought forms that we can release in meditation. The objective is to move our awareness beyond what is normal for us. We turn inward to the quiet, still place inside where, empty of our thoughts and fears, we can hear.

This can take practice. When I started, I was told to put pen to paper and begin to write. I sat down at my keyboard. I was amazed that as I wrote my question, I heard an answer coming from somewhere other than the place where my thoughts usually arise. It felt like listening rather than thinking.

I asked Michael if he had a suggestion for opening to messages.

Lilia, perhaps it would help if I share what I see you do and what works best. You first had to get over your fear of what was an unknown activity to you. A book helped you. Talking to others who communicate this way helped. The Internet was not so available when you started. There are plenty of angel experts available all over the Earth. We have been working with many, just as we have with you.

Having information helps, but the listener needs to deal with emotions or blocks that come up. You still struggle when you want a specific answer or have a significant issue and want to make sure that you are hearing our guidance correctly. It is a learning process. The listener has to be willing to do the work that allows for open communication. As you mentioned, having a strong meditation practice helps. The deeper a person is willing to go, the clearer the messages will be heard.

Since the early days, I sometimes engage through writing, usually on my laptop. Other times, I ask and get quiet. If I don't feel like opening my computer, I find a pen and paper and let the messages flow that way. Any of these methods work. Find a way that works best for you.

Be patient if it does not start immediately. You may have blocks you need to clear first.

If There Are Blocks, Be Willing to Remove Them

Even after quieting my mind and entering a meditative state, I may find my communications blocked. Rather than force it, I use a tool that came to me through reading *A Course in Miracles*.[7] It is the concept of being "willing." That state of willingness allows your angel helpers to move whatever blocks may be in your way, even those that you cannot see.

Studies suggest that the conscious mind makes up a small percentage of the total mind. The subconscious comprises the bulk of the mind, and much that is stored in the subconscious is unknown to the conscious portion. We tap into the subconscious through meditation and other focused practices. The more we bring to the conscious mind, the more control we have over our decisions and actions.

My biggest challenge in listening to angels has been to let go of my fear of being unworthy or a fear that the message might be adulterated by my ego. When I let go of fear or conditioned thought and allow the message to flow, it feels real. The words do not feel like something I would write or imagine on my own. The messages are always accompanied by a feeling of love. I often wonder why I do not take more time to let the messages come through, because the love that accompanies them is worth the experience.

Another category of blocks may be resentments or judgments you hold in your mind. Forgiveness is key for releasing them. You may wonder what forgiveness toward something or someone else has to do with communicating with an angel. Resentment and judgment can weigh us down. Forgiveness clears us of the weight and lifts our vibration. I can let go of my judgment, criticism, and complaints and forgive myself and others for perceived wrongs. In doing so, I find freedom. When I dwell on the perception of harm, it brings up anger, guilt, fear, resentment, and frustration. These keep me in downward spirals and ruts. Forgiveness helps me turn those feelings around.

In the midst of what feels like an attack or intentional harmful act, my teachers suggest that we do the best we can in each moment with the level of awareness and consciousness available to us in that moment. That concept helps us let go of unpleasant emotions toward others and ourselves. It frees us to feel love and compassion no matter the circumstances.

That does not mean that we walk around as victims with excuses, or live as perpetrators with immunity. We cannot be a victim or a perpetrator at this level of understanding. We are acting in harmony with Spirit, and that is what is real. The rest is unreal. In complete forgiveness, there is nothing to forgive.

If this seems perplexing, let me invite you to explore forgiveness at whatever level of understanding you can. See if it makes you feel lighter and more at peace as you let go and forgive.

Our blocks may not be known, but by being willing and turning our attention inward, we can begin to shift or remove them. I remember a workshop in which I was learning about crystals and tapping into how I could use them during healing sessions. I sensed that some of my gifts would require me to stretch beyond what I could imagine, and I shared that with the teacher. He asked me if I would be willing to stretch and grow into those gifts. Being asked to merely be willing took immense pressure off me. It also taught me a great lesson, because even though we may be asked to evolve beyond what we have imagined for ourselves, we never do it alone. Whether we view ourselves working with angels, Spirit, God, or whatever name we use for the divine aspect that works in us, it is a co-creative process. Stepping into the state of willingness allows us to recognize that cooperative aspect of the process.

I would like to ask the angels working with me on the book what they have to add to what I have said.

Humans put up many blocks to their connection to the angels who want to work with them. You have been working with us for years, and it still happens to you. It is like any spiritual practice—the more you spend time on it with clear intention and a willingness to let go of whatever does not serve, you will find that it becomes easier and more beneficial. Consider the practice of meditation. Many people have great difficulty spending time focused on the breath or a mantra instead of the habitual thoughts that predominate human life. The blocks vary according to the individual. For some, it is hard to sit long enough to achieve a meditative state. For some, there are physical issues—pain, discomfort, or other physical sensations—that distract from a peaceful state. For others, there are issues of fear, anxiety, or other emotions that have a strong hold on the individual's state. If they have not experienced the peaceful state of meditation, they may be distrustful of the practice. What if it uncovers additional emotions that are even harder to handle? What if the current emotions intensify? Only practice and experience can show the value. Being willing to practice and experience can help the individual understand that fears, anxieties, and other blocks can be overcome.

There are other tools to help remove blocks. Bring full awareness to your willingness to remove a block. Notice if it shows up as a constriction in your body. Is it related to a thought? A thought is usually tied to a belief that no longer serves you. The thought will trigger an emotion, and you will feel the constriction. Ask the angels to help you release that thought and any related outdated beliefs. If that does not work, ask for additional help.

Ask for Help from a Human You Trust

Even though angels are working with us for our highest good, we will often face challenges that are hard to overcome despite their help. Have you not had times when you knew there was a better way to live, but it meant letting go of a habit or belief that felt impossible to release? Did you not feel stymied, not knowing how to proceed because life felt overwhelming? In my toughest times (such as during my divorce), I needed the help of therapists. They helped me to see things about myself and my situation that I could not, and they helped me see underlying beliefs that were blocking me. One huge insight was realizing my belief that someone who loved me would never harm me. They helped me see that people have different motivations, and even those who express love may prefer control and power over love and compassion. I did not have the life experience to understand that or the maturity to master my emotions for my own protection at first. They supported me in healthy practices until I could protect myself on my own.

When I was dealing with my heartbreaks I had trouble trusting the wisdom of the angels, because it was coming through my filter, and I did not feel strong enough to know what was true. Talking to an objective third party, particularly someone trained as a therapist or a spiritual counselor, can help you toward a state where you trust what is coming through you.

Working with angels may open you up to emotions you did not know you had. When you are vulnerable you may not feel that you can trust yourself to discern what comes from conditioning and what comes from the higher realms of Spirit. Professional help may be what you need.

As we evolve, we may find that help from a teacher or mentor is crucial. We are often blind to what we most need to see in ourselves. A teacher who has travelled a path in alignment with ours can see what we cannot. They know when we are slipping into conditioned responses and teach us how to see that for ourselves. Even the most enlightened humans have had teachers to guide them.

If you do not have a teacher or mentor to help you on your path, ask your angels to help you find the one best for you. Angels are great at orchestrating the connections to those who can best help us. We do not even need to know that they are making the connections. We need only ask and pay attention to the signs and synchronicities that occur.

You may wonder if you are deficient when you need help along the way, or other judgments may arise. Let limiting thoughts go so that you can proceed on your path as easily as possible. We are here to help each other just as the angels are. Don't let pride get in the way. Why make it harder to do the good you came to do in this life?

I strongly believe that we are asked to share our unique gifts. We also need to be open to receive the unique gifts of others. That is how the flow of giving and receiving works.

We are all one, and yet we are each unique. When we have an issue to work through, we can count on someone being there to help us resolve it. If we block that help for fear that we will be considered deficient or for some other reason, we cut off the divine flow that is readily available to us. Humans can help us, and angels can help find the right humans to do so.

Step 4: Thank Them for the Guidance

Gratitude is an Essential Spiritual Practice

Gratitude is essential when working with the angelic realm. Gratitude opens our hearts. The expression of thankfulness expands our awareness to all the good that we take for granted. As we bring to mind the many ways we are blessed, even if it is as basic as "I am breathing, and I am grateful for my breath," we feel uplifted by that moment of conscious awareness and appreciation. I find that as I begin with one statement, another is close behind. "I am grateful that I have a warm house even though it is freezing outside. I am grateful that I have electricity so that I can use my laptop for writing. I am grateful that Dad went to the store so that we have oranges and apples to eat this morning." The simplest expressions of gratitude can open up our heart space and lift our mood.

Once we focus on these simple expressions of gratitude, we can go deeper, and the longer we stay with it, the deeper we go. If I start with gratitude for my breath, that leads me to gratitude for life itself, for my family and friends, and for all the things I may take for granted. I bring to mind how magnificent all of creation is and how the creative force that brought all this to be is beyond comprehension. How vast and plentiful creation is, and how small and yet blessed am I to be a part of it. This beautiful practice of appreciation and gratefulness can lead me to an ecstatic state or at least shift me from a state of worry and concern to serenity. I am breathing. All is well. I am grateful. I am gratefulness. I am great fullness.

Gratitude Is for You, Not Them

The principles of gratitude apply in working with angels. Expressing thanks for their message opens us up to receive more. Without that step, we shut down the flow. The expression of gratefulness is like magic. The angels do not need it; we need it, because it opens our hearts to fully appreciate the gifts we are given through our angelic helpers. As our hearts open wider, we can hear more clearly, feel more fully, know more definitely, and act more courageously. With a simple thought of appreciation, we flip a switch and turn on the lights, glow in the warmth of the love overflowing, and remember what we had forgotten. This light, love, and warmth are always available to us.

Step 5: Act on Their Guidance

You have reached into your heart to connect with the angels and have asked for assistance. You have opened your heart to their wisdom and listened with an open mind.

Acting is the most important step and, of course, can sometimes be the most challenging. This can require discipline, letting go of what does not serve us any longer, facing truth instead of the lies we have told ourselves, saying goodbye to friends who are no longer aligned with our purpose, or habits that hold us back.

Acting can be difficult, but what happens if we do not act? Don't expect scolding or punishment from the angels: that is not their role. We may end up scolding ourselves or feeling that we need a kick in the butt because we knew better, but angels are here to guide us, not to discipline us.

If we do not act, we become stagnant, and it may be harder to reach them. Their next piece of guidance may depend on heeding their first. They are exceedingly patient. Time does not mean to them what it does to us, and they can wait until we are ready. We will know how much time we wasted when we get around to doing what they suggested, but they will not berate us for that.

As an example, I had been writing this book in some form or other for eight years. Several times I thought I was close to getting it edited and published, but it never felt good enough. I realized that I had not listened enough to the wisdom of the angels. Much of what I did not like was what came through my thoughts rather than my inspirations and guidance. Michael and others told me that they would help me, but I did not always trust that their guidance would be available. During those times of distrust, I plunged ahead and wrote what passed through my thoughts. Much of that writing has been discarded. They asked me to focus on what I was having the most trouble with: listening. When I did that, the book was truly birthed.

Picture yourself with a bag over your shoulder, similar to the one that Santa Claus uses to bring Christmas gifts to children. Your bag holds your gifts—the ones you have not yet started sharing, the ones your angels want to help you with. As long as they exist as thoughts and messages but have not yet been accepted or acted on, they will weigh you down. Life is much harder when a bag of unfulfilled possibilities is slowing your progress. Gifts can turn into burdens. Take out a gift, a message, or a call to action, and act. You will feel so much lighter and brighter in all ways. Feel the glow? It can be as simple as taking one of your gifts out of your imaginary bag and sharing it with the world.

Discern Truth

When we receive a communication from the angelic realms, we are likely to doubt the truth of the message. It can feel foreign and unfamiliar, defying logic or reason, yet it is no less real than what we consider scientific truth. We need to learn how to discern what is true *for us*. It can take time and practice but it *is* possible to uncover our personal truth. The clearer we get on our personal truth, the closer we get to what I call "Divine Truth"—the absolute truth that I feel Buddha, Jesus, and other wise and holy (whole) ones knew.

Discernment, or clearly understanding what is true for us, is an art. It flows through inspiration and yet benefits from practice. It is an individual exercise. No one can discern for another. It may take a while to sort through related emotions, thoughts, and conditioning. It also may take several types of practices to discern the truth of something counter to what I thought before. When I get to that place of knowing, I can feel it in my body. My whole being—my emotions, thoughts, and sensations—feel aligned and congruent. When I act on that knowing, life falls into place as though it is orchestrated around that truth.

I once had a deep realization that the relationship I was in was not good for my spiritual growth. I knew I had heard that advice from my angels, because it felt true in my body. I shared it with my partner. His first response was anger. He slipped from anger to sadness, told me how much he loved me, and cried. He promised that he would fully support me on my spiritual path. I desperately wanted to believe that he loved me and would support me on my path. I ignored the guidance that felt so true and gave this love another chance.

Years later, I came to the same realization: the relationship was never going to support me on my path and I had to let it go. I moved on to my next level of transformation and spiritual evolution. Had I wasted the years in between? I don't believe so. Some part of me needed the experiences I had while I did it "my way" instead of the "higher way" of my guidance, yet I know that the original guidance was true. I was not ready to follow it. It was a choice point, and I chose a detour. I ended up in the same place years later. I know that the original guidance was trying to get me there faster, but I needed to learn additional lessons along the way. I have no regrets. He loved me as much as he could. I grew to no longer need love in the desperate way I had needed it for most of my life. I could have taken the shortcut that Spirit was providing me, but I chose the long route instead. This is all part of the discernment process. It is not enough to know it to be true: we need the courage and confidence to act on it.

Sometimes we are not ready, but our allies in Spirit are patient. They wait until we are willing, to help us. I have never felt criticism from my allies for not being ready, only love and encouragement. When I have an opening, they are there to assist.

We may have to grow into guidance. As we do, and the more we act on the guidance we discern as truth, we realize that we are better off doing it sooner rather than later, even if it feels impossible. No matter how we respond, we are loved and supported.

If my life does not flow easily from a decision based on discernment, I take another look. Perhaps I did not see something clearly. Maybe I missed a part of the message. What if the answer is right but the timing is wrong? To begin a discernment practice, I use meditative or focused breathing. I stay aware of thoughts as they appear and observe how my body feels. Is there a tightness somewhere? Is that tightness trying to tell me something? If I breathe into the tightness, does it dissolve? Does another thought arise that moves the energy or loosens it, bringing an "aha" moment?

When a thought appears, you can notice how it feels in your body. Do you feel at peace? Is your energy flowing, or is there a constriction somewhere? If you feel like you are in a stuck place, take your awareness to where the flow is jammed and be present to it. Ask it a question. Is it trying to tell you something? Is there another way to look at this situation?

I visualize life force streaming through my body. I visualize it as light. It is what connects us to Source in each moment. By bringing our awareness to it, we can more consciously interact with it and co-create our ideas, visions, and all aspects of life. The light is our basic, vital, life energy that flows through each of as it is does through all living things. It is stored in things that are not considered living such as crystals and other rock forms. It is stored in all matter, for matter is merely dense energy.

Each of us has the innate ability to work with that vital life energy, in a discernment exercise, to practice the art of knowing within our body. As we attune ourselves to that inner knowing, we attune ourselves to the higher frequencies. That is when we become aware of our callings, our yearnings to be and do at higher frequencies. As we develop our abilities to discern, we find that it is easier to stay in alignment with our Higher Self. Our vibrations no longer wobble or become diffused and dissonant. There is an alignment and strength in the alignment. As we align fully at our core level, we evolve. It is as simple—and as difficult—as that.

In a conversation with Michael in 2009, he spoke about the discernment process. I began the discussion by talking about my concerns about global changes. Our economy had taken a big hit in 2008, and things were looking grim. There was apocalyptic talk as we got closer to 2012. Some thought that the Mayans predicted the end of time to coincide with the end of their calendar, even though more informed scholars tried to get the word out that it reflected the beginning of a new set of cycles, not the end of the world. After I expressed my concerns, Michael had reassuring words about our impending transformation and what tools to bring to it.

Lilia, you are on the right track. It is important that each person open up to his or her divine guidance in whatever form it takes. This is a time for transformation. Transformation is not just change, although there are changes that take place in the transformational process. Transformation takes a person into unknown territory. It can feel unfamiliar and give rise to fear, but when people are connected to their divine guidance, they can trust that they are moving in the best direction for their evolution. There are no maps for this kind of transformation. There is only the inner guidance system that each person has that allows the inner knowing of what is truest for that individual. It is a skill that is innate but strengthened through practice. You have been developing yours, and becoming more adept and confident as a result.

By using various discernment practices I have come to understand that my body knows more than my head or my heart. Surprisingly it is through communicating with the body that we can get all three aligned most efficiently. When the three are aligned, we enter the flow of life in a consistent manner.

"Muscle testing" is a method that shows how the physical body communicates its wisdom (some call it "Applied Kinesiology"). I have witnessed muscle testing by a few health practitioners. They use complex procedures to make the process more scientific and reliable, but there are simpler techniques that people can use for themselves. A friend who teaches energy medicine demonstrates shifts in energy by having someone hold out an arm horizontally. She tests the energy by pushing near the wrist while the person tries to hold the arm firm. If the energy is low, the arm falls easily. If the energy is positive, the arm stays firm. The same test can be used for a yes or a no answer to a question. A yes answer will have the positive energy that allows the arm to stay firm, while a no answer will cause the arm to fall easily. There are variations on this practice. Another friend tests with both arms held at an angle in front of the person's body. She can sense a yes or a no with a slight movement of one of the arms.

I have learned to use my fingers to test myself for a yes or no. I test to see what the energy feels like for a yes and test again for a no. I ask my question and see if my body says yes or no.

This type of feedback from my body is useful for many things. For example, you can muscle test for the best type of apple to buy! Or if you trying a new food, there may be three brands with the same ingredients, but they may not have been produced with the same care. Through muscle testing, you can discern which is best for you. I like to use my whole body, and I hold whatever I am testing in my hands. I stand straight and notice which way my body wants to go. If it naturally moves forward, I know that the food will likely be good for me. If my body starts to move backward, I will put it back on the shelf. Your body may move differently than mine. Try it with products that you know are good or bad for you and see how your body reacts. Try it with products you don't know and see what your body tells you. This recommendation comes with a caveat: this is not science. This is not infallible, so do not use it for something that could be harmful to you.

Like any discernment exercise, muscle testing takes practice. What works for me might not work in the same way for you, but if you take time to pay attention to what your body is telling you, you might be surprised by its wisdom. I do not suggest that anyone use this tool on a major decision without testing the decision in other ways. Muscle testing is an intuitive art form, and it takes practice and experience in validation to become confident and capable in its use. However, it is an important tool for discernment of one's truth.

Know Your Truth and Be Open to the Truth of Others

Whatever discernment methods you use, the important thing is to find practices that help you discover your truth. When that becomes difficult, be open to assistance. Sometimes sounding out an idea with a good friend will help you see that you are missing a piece of the puzzle. Other times it may require the services of a trained professional. I am a strong believer in talking to a trusted counselor or therapist when I have huge life decisions to make. I know that the responsibility for the discernment is mine, but I also know that I have blind spots that others can help me see. Professionals are trained to do that.

As we understand our personal truth, we need to approach it with humility. Feeling we have a monopoly on truth is what creates conflicts between religions and leads to wars. Personal truth is diverse. By being humble in our discernment and respecting the process and practices of others, we open up to a deeper and more powerful understanding of our own truth.

One process that has helped me understand how discernment works is group consensus building. In this process, the group does a centering exercise through meditation and breathing techniques. Each member of the group goes within and discerns what he or she feels is the best decision for the group, and each shares the result of the discernment. The group begins with various results and takes that diversity back into meditation. If each member is willing to speak from a place of personal truth as the process unfolds, a decision arises that may be beyond what any one person first imagined. It will contain the inspiration of the group and a synthesis of the diverse views. Sometimes one or two feel strongly about a counterview. If the group respects the process, it will find something in that counterview that will enhance and uplift the final decision.

By participating in this type of activity I have learned some tough lessons about discernment. In one instance, a governing board of an organization was trying to make a decision about hiring a leader. It had taken a long time to get to that point, and the members of the board were tired. When we went into group discernment, I sensed that the group wanted to be done with the process. There were a few in the group who felt strongly that things would work out no matter what decision was made. I had misgivings but did not speak up. Instead of respecting my inner truth and sharing it with the group, I allowed the views and feelings of the others to prevail. The decision did not work out, and it was a divisive experience for the organization. I learned that each person must speak up and trust their inner guidance while respecting what others are discerning. There is a balance in that process that leads to a higher level of understanding. It leads to personal growth for everyone: each person is required to get in touch with his or her personal truth, respect another's viewpoint, and trust that in the synthesis of the diversity, inspirational results can be achieved.

I am on a board of a nonprofit organization that uses consensus for our decision- making process. Sometimes we require longer periods, and thus postpone decisions for further discussion or reflection. However, because discernment is central to our decision-making process, we have a greater sense of support in each decision. We also feel that Spirit has helped us achieve the decision, particularly when there are diverse opinions among the members.

Action Requires Trust in Their Guidance

For me to act on the guidance of my angels, I have to trust that the message is true. That is when the work of discernment is so necessary. As you exercise your discerning skills you come to know what is true and what is your imagination or ego at play.

As I prepared to retire in 2010, I asked the angels if that was the best time. I knew that there was a part of me that wanted to do something different. How could I know through their messages that it was time for me to take that leap? It had huge financial consequences. I repeatedly went into discernment. What was true? Was fear of the unknown keeping me from following my guidance?

After months of listening, discerning, worrying, and wondering, I knew that it was the right choice. I did not know how I would make it work. I talked to my supervisors and let them know I would be leaving. I took the leap and it allowed me to take my momentous trip to Bolivia. Even though I went back to the same work and had to figure out other pieces to my financial puzzle, I was able to work part-time. I used my time off to write and prepare for my final move and the work I felt called to do.

I had to reach a point where I trusted the guidance I received. I took my time. It is important that you get to that same point of trust. If it is true guidance, the angels will find ways to make it clear to you. When the signs show up, pay attention. The angels are trying to get beyond your doubts, and they are here to help you even when you resist.

Summon Courage if Action Seems Scary

Acting on the guidance of angels will often seem scary. It usually involves change, and the unknown brings up fears. I have had several teachers tell me that if I want to grow, I have to embrace being uncomfortable and scared. I cannot let fear stop me or I will never accomplish what is most important for me. Fear can actually be an indicator that I am headed in the right direction. It is just new and unfamiliar territory.

When fears come up, I discuss them with someone I trust such as a coach, a counselor, or a trusted friend. They can help me discover the source of the fear. Is it based on conditioning or an old wound from childhood? Is it the spookiness of what I don't know? Maybe it is not the right time.

Over time, I have become more comfortable with trusting the guidance I receive and moving into the fearful unknown as I act on it. I let my emotions be my guide. Even if I feel fear, there will be excitement and anticipation as well. If I start to feel constricted, I take a step back and ask again, "Is it time? Am I ready?" They will let me know.

When Action Becomes Difficult, Begin Again with Step One

Sometimes I feel stuck, I back off, or stop listening. Whatever happens, it is okay. I can begin again. I can go into the quiet and begin the process again, asking, "Are you sure this is what I am supposed to be doing? Why does it not feel right? What am I missing?"

The beauty of this art is that there isn't any wrong way of doing it. We can forget our angels for years, and when we remember, they are right there waiting for us to ask for their assistance. They don't respond by saying, "Where were you?" They don't need to because they know, and they love us anyway.

CHAPTER 4

Angels Help Us Live Our Soul's Purpose

Angels know our soul's purpose and can help us live it. We each have a unique way in which we are meant to show up in this life. When on track with that purpose, I feel fulfilled—full of vibrancy, full of aliveness, full of all of the good things in life: joy, excitement, anticipation, curiosity, and a sense of play. I may encounter some fear mixed in, because when I am on purpose, I am usually moving into unknown territory. As you connect to your unique soul's purpose, you will be going where no one else has gone. You will be doing what you have never done before. That can be scary.

Help with Identifying Our Soul's Purpose

I tuned in to my soul's purpose fifteen years ago. I had a vague sense of what it was—to be helpful, spiritual, to be the best person I could be—but nothing specific. I chose a career as a lawyer and felt that I was being helpful in that work. Instead of working as a typical lawyer, I found drafting legislation that had the potential to become state law intriguing and satisfying. I enjoyed figuring out how to find the right words and draft a written solution to a problem the state legislation was trying to solve. My specialties were pension law and tax law. The work required me to continually learn about new issues and craft language that would resolve them. However, as much as I enjoyed my job, I knew there was a way that I could serve more fully using my mental faculties and my spiritual abilities.

As a child, I was inspired to be a missionary, but I had a naïve understanding of what that meant. Aunt Mabel, my favorite aunt, served as my mentor when I was young and she loved to tell me stories of missionaries she knew who were spreading what they considered the good news of their beliefs to those who had no access to that knowledge. Albert Schweitzer was one such person I remember her telling me about. I was impressed that someone was willing to make such personal sacrifices, to go to remote areas in Africa to provide medical care and other services to the poor. He was so dedicated to protecting life that he did not kill insects. That seemed so compassionate to me as a child that I never forgot it.

Aunt Mabel also told me stories about Billy Graham. Although he was an evangelist in the United States and not a missionary in a foreign country, he was passionate about his beliefs and dedicated his life to "saving souls." I found that type of belief fascinating. I attended one of his gatherings and was mesmerized by the revival-type gathering at a stadium in Philadelphia. I even walked to the stage in front of thousands of people to declare Jesus as my lord and savior and "be born again." I considered going to a college that specialized in training missionaries and ministers. Aunt Mabel said she would help fund my training should I decide to take that route.

Sadly, my aunt died when I was twelve. Without her influence I no longer aspired to be a missionary. I even began to question my Christian beliefs. I went to a secular college where I studied math and pre-law. I left the Protestant church of my youth because its explanations of the Bible were too narrow for me. I studied other faiths and spiritual disciplines and explored the Muslim faith of my ex-husband. Nothing satisfied my inquisitive mind, which was searching for a deeper spiritual truth. Eventually I found a church that embraced many spiritual faiths while being focused on prayer and the principles of truth. It felt like home as soon as I entered its sanctuary where the congregants were meditating before the service. Meditation was a key spiritual practice there and that allowed me to open up to what felt true to me, even if it was not supported by traditional religious doctrine.

It was in that environment that I was finally able to open more fully to the angelic messages coming through me.

It was also in that church that I began more clearly to understand my purpose. One day the minister held a workshop on discovering spiritual gifts and purpose. She asked us to list things we enjoyed doing and things we felt we did well. She then led us in a meditation in which we asked the question in the silence, "What is my soul's purpose?" The message that came to me was "Your purpose is to bring heaven on earth." I was not expecting that. It seemed to come out of nowhere. As others shared what came to them, things like teaching children, working with nature, or designing unique living spaces, I felt that my revelation was grandiose. The other purposes that were shared were more specific and practical. Even though I spoke it aloud, it felt too large to take on at that time. My guidance in the meditation did not specify how I was to accomplish it and left me in a quandary. Even so, I could not deny that I felt a sense of truth in the message I received.

I feel that my angels gave me that message, because it did not come through my thinking process. Even though I sometimes confuse the two, I now know the difference. The message came through as a communication, not a thought, which would have sounded more like "I *think* I should bring heaven on earth!" That would have been an ego creation (and would have felt like it). The message I received felt like an inspiration, a goal so big that I could not have thought it myself but one that resonated deep inside. It scared me in a good way.

I have come to understand that heaven is here on earth and in the present moment—we need only become aware of it. There is no "bringing" to be done other than peeling away any illusion that it does not exist or releasing a belief that it exists elsewhere. Awareness of this truth can take work, because we are highly conditioned to believe that heaven is not available in a human body, even though Jesus is quoted as saying, "... the Kingdom of God is within you."[8]

Understanding that heaven is available to us here and now, and living it, is an ongoing process. I need to bring the awareness of heaven to myself and then to others. As I become open to that awareness, the love and light of heaven flow in. I feel joy and a natural state of happiness that needs no cause for these wonderful feelings. As I share this awareness with others, I feel on purpose.

A few months after the workshop where I identified my soul's purpose, I had a communication with Archangel Michael. I was struggling with a few issues and started a dialogue with him. Michael asked me to focus on what I wanted. That question had been extremely helpful at key points in my life. I answered that I wanted to feel that I was on my path without distractions and fulfilling my purpose. He asked me what I thought was my purpose. When I said bringing heaven on earth, he asked me what that meant to me. He kept asking me questions until I felt clearer about what that meant and how I would accomplish that lofty goal. It was helpful to have that dialogue with him to gain greater clarity.

I have come to know that when I feel I am on purpose, I am balanced and full of energy. I may have the same issues, but they seem inconsequential because of that fullness. Life flows. I don't feel like I am swimming upstream or pushing the river. Smiles and laughter come more easily.

Help with Clarifying Our Soul's Purpose

The Universe has been supportive in keeping me on track. Naturally, the angels keep reminding me, but big events in my life have left no doubt in my mind. In 2007, I was given a great opportunity to go to Peru. How that happened was most certainly the work of Spirit. During the trip, my connection with Michael deepened tremendously.

A friend was spearheading the tour. To generate interest, she suggested a raffle for a ticket that would include the basics for the trip: food, lodging, transportation while there, and the basic cost for guides. Tipping, transportation there, and any extras were additional, but the basic trip cost was a significant prize. The raffle was to benefit a nonprofit organization, and the board members were to sell a minimum number of tickets. When it came time to turn in the tickets we sold, I could not think of anyone who would want to go to Peru other than my friends who were also selling tickets. I decided to purchase all of the tickets I was assigned to sell, and then I added in an additional amount, so the check I wrote was for $333.00. A triple three is a spiritual number that I relate to Christ consciousness. As I wrote the check and put it in the envelope, I said to myself, *If the Universe wants me to go on this trip, I will win.*

On the day of the raffle I was sitting in the circle of attendees and watched a board member pull a ticket out of the basket. She called my name. I remembered what I had said when I wrote the check and realized the Universe wanted me to go. I still had to come up with a significant amount of money to pay for airfare and other items, but I could not say no to such a gift from Spirit.

The other travelers turned out to be all women, and an aspect of the trip was to reflect on our lives and spiritual growth as we explored the sacred sites of Peru. Daily yoga sessions helped us reach deep meditative states. We participated in a few ceremonies by local shamans. The high point of the trip was taking two trips to Machu Picchu, one of them on the winter solstice.

If you have never been to Machu Picchu, put it on your bucket list. It is a beautiful place, but more than that, it has a sacred energy to it that is powerful even to those who are not sensitive to energy fields. We held a beautiful ceremony in a circle on one of the flatter spaces. I had an intense experience of veils opening, love streaming down, and being grounded in the earth. I hugged everyone in the group, because I wanted them to have a sense of the bliss I was feeling.

Each spot on the grounds of Machu Picchu holds different energy. From what our guide told us, each area was designed for a specific purpose. Most were for a particular sacred ritual. Other areas had been used as living quarters or for growing food. Since we there on the solstice, we were able to see one of the most amazing parts of the design. At sunrise, the sun was in direct alignment with a hole carved in one of the stone walls. On other days, the alignment is not exact. It was magnificent to watch the sunlight streaming through that window. Our guide told us that the placement of the window was only one part of the design that showed comprehensive knowledge of the movements of the sun and stars, not to mention precise alignment of the structures. No one knows how the Incas were able to construct the walls with such precision.

It was a magical, mystical place and the energy took me deep into my soul. Later that day, I was sitting with a friend on one of the rock formations that carried water from the top to lower levels of the place. We understood it to be where sacred bathing rituals took place. I sat there and tuned in to Michael. Here are some excerpts from his messages.

June 21, 2007, Winter Solstice on Machu Picchu

Each person can be a conduit of energy from heaven to earth and back again. Consider the figure eight. It represents the flow of energy from heaven to earth and back again in an infinite cycle. That is why the infinity sign is the number eight on its side.

By opening oneself to the light of the heavens and the heavenly bodies, one can start the infinite flow. Then by connecting to Mother Earth, one can ground the flow and get it reenergized if the energy gets stuck in the body.

After writing that in my journal, we were asked to move. We did not realize that as a sacred bathing spot, tourists were not to sit there. When we returned to the hotel where we were staying, I continued listening to Michael.

Another way to bring heaven to earth is to remember a wise old tree you have a heart connection to. The large branches reach up to the heavens for sustenance in the form of light. The light is absorbed through the leaves in a chemical process.

There is a flow of energy down the trunk into the roots where the nourishment of Mother Earth is absorbed and sucked up the tree to the leaves in an osmotic process. So it is with humans. The light of God enters into the crown chakra, travels through the body, through the feet, and is rooted in Mother Earth if the individual allows it. The individual can then sense the energy of Mother Earth through the feet, up the body, and through the crown. And once again the infinite flow begins.

One other message from Michael on that life-changing trip was the following.

> *As you connect heaven with earth, you will feel the colors of the rainbow. You will not only see them, but you will feel them throughout your body. Pay attention in the moment, and see how in each moment there is movement and change. In each moment, there is the preciousness and beauty of that moment. Feel and see it in your body. Feel and see it in the world around you. Feel and see the connection between heaven and earth.*

The day between the two trips to the top, we were given the opportunity to go to a waterfall at the base of Machu Picchu. We had to walk along railroad tracks to get there. It was a beautiful spot, and we did not encounter other tourists. It felt refreshing and renewing, particularly when going into the water under the falls. There were flowers everywhere. It was breathtaking.

On the way back, I found myself walking alone on the railroad, contemplating what this trip meant to me and for my life's purpose. I knew that I wanted to leave my work as a lawyer and begin a Reiki practice. As I walked, I felt Michael's energy. It was as if his energy merged with mine. I started moving my arms as if they were angel wings swinging, the tips outlining an infinity symbol. Michael asked me to remember this feeling so that I could take it into my healing practice and to know what it feels like to bring heaven on earth. It was magical.

I felt totally supported by Michael in living my soul's purpose. Having it confirmed so strongly in that magical place in Peru made it clear that connecting heaven and earth, and helping others to do so, was what I came in this life to accomplish. I am still figuring out how, but helping others to listen to angels is a piece of it.

The help we can receive to discover and achieve our soul's purpose is the most important reason for learning how to communicate with angels. We have only this time to do what we came here to do. We may have other lifetimes to do other things, but we came into this body at this time for a specific, unique purpose. Why not ask the angels to help us do it? They cannot do it for us, and we cannot do it when we pass over to the Spirit realm.

We need the most help in the daily living of our purpose. Daily practices help keep us on track, and meditation and journaling are key practices. Whatever practices you use, invite the angels to help you. You may be surprised how support shows up for you when you do.

I sometimes forget and get busy with other aspects of my life. When I return to my communications through meditation and journaling, it is as if I never stopped. A few months ago, I restarted my practice of journaling my communications with Michael. I was feeling some guilt and remorse for having gotten away from it for a while. Michael lovingly reminded me that for any practice, one starts in the present moment, saying, *Let the guilt and fear go and bring your love and attention to the present moment.* He reminded me that this is what I teach to others. I had to smile.

When I take the time to check in each day, whether through meditation or journaling, I receive a "course correction" for the places in life that are out of alignment. I receive reminders of what I know but may have forgotten, such as beginning in the present moment and letting go of negative emotions that pull me into the past or future. I know that living in the now is the only way to create what I desire in my life. I have written about it and taught it to students. I sometimes forget, so it is so wonderful to have angel allies to remind me.

Are you on purpose? Have you identified your soul's purpose? Use the steps in chapter 3 for the AOLTA process to help you wherever you are, to bring you into the present moment and course correct if need be. If you forget what they are, use the acronym to help you remember: Ask, Open your heart, Listen, Thank them, and Act. You will find that your angels will be delighted to help you stay on track with what you came into this life to do. When you forget, they will remind you. If you are unsure, they will help you gain the clarity you need. If you are feeling guilt, shame, or fear, or are stuck in a rut, they will help you let it all go so that you can be who you came here to be.

CHAPTER 5

Opening Up to Our Own Angel Energy

When I started learning about angels, I was told that they are a separate life form that have not lived as humans. I heard from different experts on this subject and about the concept of "earth angels." Earth angels are humans who embody angel energy. They often appear temporarily to help in a situation and then leave. Diana Cooper recounts several such stories in her book, *A Little Light on Angels.*[9] The existence of earth angels is hard to prove because they disappear once they have done their good deed. However, the many stories about how beings in human form inexplicably disappear after saving a life or doing something miraculous make the idea credible and worth consideration.

There is a related concept that some of us embody angel energy yet live otherwise normal lives, and thus are a different type of earth angel. I have been told that I am one on several occasions. I was not sure what to make of this, but when it came from a gifted intuitive who gives angel readings, I decided to pay attention.

The reading occurred when we were both exhibitors at a conference. I was giving Reiki sessions next to her booth where she was giving angel readings. When we both had a break I asked for a reading. She said, "You know you are an angel, don't you? That is what they are telling me." My eyes filled with tears. Even though I had been told that before and part of me believed it, I denied the truth of it. After that reading, I decided to enter into a discernment process around it to understand what was true for me.

You may be wondering if this could be true for you and, if so, how to distinguish truth from the workings of ego. Remember that the ego works in two ways. It projects a self-image that is either larger or smaller than we truly are. We feel puffed up like a peacock or deflated as a spent balloon. The ego is trying to protect us, but our truth is in between.

As I consider the idea that I embody angel energy, I have two reactions: "Wow, that is awesome and huge—how wonderful," and "Wow, that is awesome and huge—no way!"

When the idea occurs to me, whether as a result of my own contemplation or from an angel reading by an expert, I recognize there is something about it that feels true. There is a resonance in my energy field. My internal truth meter sends out signals, such as chills or my hairs standing on end. Next my fears take hold. I tell myself, *This cannot be. I am way too flawed. I am not worthy. Angels don't lose their temper and get angry. Angels don't make bad choices around love. Angels are perfect. How can I embody angel energy? I am so imperfect.*

Because of my fears and limiting thoughts, I may consider the idea many times, reject it, and move on to my human way of living. Even after hearing it from the angel expert, I was unable to hold the awareness in my body, all the while writing this book about listening to angels!

One morning while in meditation, I reflected on a beautiful relationship I had with a friend. We had been travel buddies on trips to sacred sites around the world and to conferences with fellow light workers, partners in teaching classes on sacred mysteries, cohorts in guiding the nonprofit organization she founded around the concept of transformation, and friends. A question came to mind as to why someone so gifted had allowed me to remain such a close friend and ally on our many adventures. We had just returned from a writing retreat in which I saw her share her many gifts that I do not have. She has been such a teacher and mentor for me and yet it has also felt that we have a very mutual appreciation for each other. She has told me many times that my friendship and companionship mean a lot to her. I asked my angels in meditation, "What is the role I play for her, because I certainly don't have many of the gifts she has?"

The answer that came to me was:

You are serving as an earth angel to her. You are reminding her of who she is. In the same way, she is reminding you of who you are. That is why it has been so important for the two of you to travel and teach together, while still developing your individual skills and expertise.

In that moment I realized that it was important for me to explore what it was that led me to keep rejecting that truth in my life. If I am an earth angel, I also am quite human. Perhaps they are not mutually exclusive, yet I have been holding the belief that they were.

The ego part of me that prefers me to stay small and in the background, the proverbial wallflower, has given me many reasons for not believing it. Who am I to claim that? Think of what people who know me will say. "Are you kidding me? She thinks she is an earth angel? Do you know what she did the other day, month, year? She is so full of herself. She is way out of line."

What if it is not as uncommon as we think to be an earth angel? What if you have been drawn to this book and to the art of listening to angels because you have angel energy inside you, asking for recognition? Does that scare you? Does it excite you? Does it intrigue you?

What if being an earth angel is no big deal? Do you know how many earth angels there are? Does anyone? What if our human consciousness is just now opening up to the understanding that angels can live human lives? What if, as we each open up to our soul and our true identity, we begin recognizing that we have angel energy as well as the human soul energy we have identified with? What does that mean for us?

As I open up to this understanding, I feel a call to be the best me I can be, whatever that is. My guiding angels are telling me to let go of the stigma or the image of what being an earth angel might mean. We are not to put anyone else on a pedestal. We serve best if we connect to our unique spark of light and radiate that into the world.

Let me allow you hear it directly from the angels who are speaking to me in this moment.

It is time to get over it. Being an earth angel is no big deal. So many of you have incarnated on earth. We have been calling you to wake up to it. You keep living your lives in denial. Even when your counselors, advisors, angel experts, psychics, mediums, and media icons tell you that earth angels exist and you are one, you go back to the lies of your life and stay miserably unfulfilled, off purpose, working in mundane jobs, and complaining about how unhappy you are. Get over it. The earth needs you to embody your angel energy. Stop rejecting it. Ground it. Live it. Embrace it. Radiate it. The time is now. Do you not understand what it will mean if you do this? How does one feel when one encounters angel energy, even when seen as external? Is it not all about love, joy, peace, and all of the attributes human are searching for? What would it feel like to embody angel energy? Could it be anything other than love, peace, and joy?

Tell your egos to stop worrying. Tell your egos that it is time for your soul to call the shots. Your soul knows your angel connection. Your soul knows that you came into this life to bring angel energy into awareness and embodiment.

What is the downside of this? Are you afraid of what others will think? Are you afraid that people will think you are crazy or delusional? What purpose does that serve?

I am telling you that being an earth angel is no big deal, because there are so many of you. I am also telling you that being an earth angel is a big deal, because it is who you are. If you deny the truth of who you are, why live?

Who are you? Are you your body? Are you your soul? Are you your ego? Are you all of that and more?

We are here to help you answer these questions. Some of them do not have complete answers and in some ways are unanswerable except in the process of asking. The asking brings you closer to your truth. As you get closer to your truth, you get closer to Truth with the capital letter "T" that indicates something beyond human understanding.

We are here to help you with everything, but you are here to live your life in your body. A truth that cannot be denied is that human bodies die. Time and bodies are connected. What that means is up for each of you to understand. What will you do with your time in your body? Will you continue to live a life of lies or will you live a life of truth as best you can discern it?

Back to the understanding of living your life embodying earth angel energy. How could that hurt? How could embodying that level of love, peace, and joy harm anyone?

We understand that like many spiritual concepts, this seems simple but is hard to do. We ask you to take this seriously so that you understand how important your answers are. Your life is important. Each life is important. Help humanity to understand that by first understanding it yourself. Who are you?

This is an age-old question that humans love to avoid answering truthfully. Are you courageous enough to explore your answer?

Wow. Thank you. Thank you all. Thank you Michael, in particular, because I know you have been trying to get me to understand the truth of my life and the importance of life in a human body so that I can share it with others. You have been so patient with me and you have been working with so many of us. Even those who have not had a direct encounter know that you are working through others all over the world.

Take some time to go into meditation and ask yourself, with the assistance of your angels and perhaps your own angel energy, who you are. What is important for you to do while you have time in this body you have been given? There may be no sense of time in the Spirit realm, but time is a factor for human life. It may be different than we understand, but it plays an unmistakable role in mind, body, and the spirit connection of human existence. Quiet your mind, focus on your breath, and when ready, ask yourself, "Who am I?" When you are ready, write down your answers, and take them into contemplation each day. The answers you receive are part of the process of living life in this body. Keep asking. Keep answering. The angels will help.

If your personal guidance is that you are not an earth angel and this idea does not resonate for you, that is fine. What is important is that you determine what is true for you and your soul's way of showing up as you in this world.

As I was doing research for this chapter, I looked through my journal entries over the years. I came upon an entry from 2002. That year I was working with the book *Sacred Contracts* by Carolyn Myss.[10] One of the archetypes that I related to was the angel. When I asked my angels why I was drawn to it, they said:

Because you are one of us. You are to be our human messenger to let people know we are here to serve. We are real. We are not just imaginary or historic beings.

When I asked myself a question from the book, "How do I serve my contracts with other people?" the answer was:

You agreed to come into this world together to usher in the new world, a heaven on earth. We are to remind you of that commitment. It starts with finding that commitment in your heart, your home, your family, and your relationships. It will extend to your selected community, your larger community, and the world. Think big. Think outside the box you have felt confined in, and know that we are here to help.

I am amazed that so many years ago, angels were inspiring me to accept my angel energy and live my purpose. Thankfully, I had recorded this in my journal to remind me of how long ago they told me this, even though I could not accept it at that time. It took a lot of work to accept it and fully understand that they are here to help me. They are also here to help you. I hope it will not take so long for you to claim it for yourself.

PART II

OPENING UP TO GUIDANCE
FROM OTHERS IN SPIRIT REALM

The principles for the art of listening to angels are applicable to listening to others in the Spirit realm. Although going beyond angelic communications can require greater discernment skills, I have found three types of communication beneficial. First, there is the possibility of communicating with loved ones who have transitioned from the physical into Spirit. Communicating with them can be comforting, and it happens naturally to many people. It may take some practice to feel that the communication is real and not imagined, but it is common for people to talk about how they bring their mother or spouse to mind and talk to them as if they are alive.

Secondly, there are beings that are different than angels called "Ascended Masters." Some are described as gods or goddesses in various cultures. This type of communication is similar to that with angels, but since some of them are not represented in the sacred texts of the Abrahamic religions (Judaism, Christianity, and Islam), this type of communication might be more controversial. I have found great value in discovering the gifts and messages of various Ascended Masters and other beings of light and love.

A third type of communication is with the fairy or elemental realm. I am not as familiar with this type of communication, but I have had a few significant experiences, including one as I was completing the writing of this book. I felt that they were asking me to include them here, so I have.

One difference between communication with angels and communication with others is that a higher level of discernment is necessary. There are beings in Spirit who are at levels of evolution that may not be in alignment with your highest good, so it is best to avoid spending time with them. I am not suggesting that you need to be fearful in this regard, but take the following precautions.

1. If the communication does not feel loving, end it.

2. Be clear on your intentions and setting the space. Ask Archangel Michael to protect you during any communications.

3. Surround yourself with the energy of angels first. Ask them to help you create a field around you of love and light.

4. Check your energy field regularly. Are your chakras clear? Are there any blocks in your energy field? If you do not know how to work with your energy field and chakras, learn how so that you can maintain your vibration at the highest levels.

5. If you do not feel good for any reason after an encounter, seek professional help from someone who works with spiritual energy such as a Reiki practitioner, energy medicine healer, acupuncturist, minister, or spiritual counselor. You want someone who is adept at reading energy fields and clearing them.

I list these precautions because it is important to feel safe and protected. I always ask Archangel Michael to look after me. If I feel scared or concerned, I ask him to intervene. By using these precautionary steps, you will create the safe space in which to do what you feel guided to do. Remember that love is the most powerful force. That is why angels are so powerful. They embody a pure form of love and protect us with it when asked to do so.

Why explore beyond the angelic realm if there are potential dangers? For me, communicating with loved ones in the Spirit realm is extremely comforting. It helps me understand more fully what to expect when I no longer live in a human body, and it allows those who have transitioned to continue being of service. If we deny their continued existence or our ability to communicate with them, they cannot impart their wisdom and love to us. Why cut off the flow? Why cause them to feel dead to us? Death is a mirage that humans have created to cause separation from the oneness that connects us all. Our loved ones can teach us differently.

Communication with Ascended Masters and other light beings, including fairies and elementals, is only an enhancement to communication with angels. However, it is more controversial, because not everyone believes these beings exist or, if they do, that they have any value within the constructs of their belief system. That is why I stress a greater level of discernment. If these types of communication do not resonate with you, let them go. Do not try to pursue them. I include these other light beings in this book because my life has been enriched by their presence.

CHAPTER 6

Communicating with Loved Ones
Is Comforting

I f we can communicate with loved ones, we find comfort and solace that they are okay and that we have not lost our connection.

One of my closest friends, Zemaya, spent the last nine months of her life battling cancer. We believed she could turn it around until her last week, but she let go and made her transition. I grieved deeply; she was a friend I could always confide in. We connected regularly. We loved to talk about books we were reading and inspirations from our morning meditations. Sometimes we started with whatever was troubling us that day and helped each other look at it from a different perspective. She was like a sister. We gave each support, love, honest feedback, and brutal honesty. We could count on each other to tell the truth no matter what.

We wanted to grow old together. We wanted to teach classes, hold retreats, travel, and have fun. Now she is no longer here in physical form, but she is still present in my life. She helped another friend and I plan her celebration of life service. As we considered what she would like—she left no instructions other than where she wanted it to be held—the pieces came together beautifully. Much of what I said during the service came from notes she sent me by email a year before. Ideas popped into my head that I knew came from her. Another friend suggested getting balloons, because she always added an element of fun to the events she hosted. As I was picking out the colors I felt her remind me of the blues and oranges she loved. I kept the arrangement in my living room for months afterward. They looked like the things that she loved to have around her, and it was comforting to have them around me.

Another way that I have felt her presence is through the sound of geese. One of her favorite poems was "Wild Geese" by Mary Oliver. We printed the poem on the back of the programs we handed out at the service.

When it was over, I went to our community beach to connect with nature and allow some of my stuffed emotions to bubble up and clear. A huge flock of geese greeted me. I took a video of them so that I would not forget. The next day I went to another beach area that she and I had visited, and two geese swam by. Immediately after that, I went to the grocery store and I noticed that the cart I chose had a particular squeak. It sounded like the two geese I had just seen. I felt that Zemaya was letting me know she was still present with me. The squeak made me laugh.

Because I can feel Zemaya's presence so strongly, my grief is easier to handle. I can hear her responses when I ask a question. That is, I can hear her in my inner ear, the way I hear my angels. I find great comfort in that. I know she is happy. She wanted to live, but she loves the life she has now. As I tune into her, she encourages me to let people know how beautiful life beyond earth is. There is so much love where she is, and I can feel it through her.

If I were not open to hearing and feeling her presence, I would be overcome by the loss. I can't imagine what it would be like. I am so grateful that I have opened up my heart and mind to hear and feel her. I recommend this practice for anyone who has lost a loved one. If that seems impossible, seek a gifted communicator with Spirit. There are many who have learned the art and can connect you if you have trouble doing it yourself. Being able to communicate with those who have crossed the veil leads to an expanded view of how life continues after physical death. How can we not feel more love and light in our lives when we know there is so much more after this lifetime? How can we not feel happier if we know that our loved ones are in a good place, happy, and filled with love beyond what we know here on earth?

When my mom passed over seven years ago, my sisters and brother seemed to grieve much more deeply than I did. I wondered about that. Was I blocking the grief? Was I in denial? Did they have a stronger relationship with her than I did? None of those explanations seemed accurate. I sensed her in Spirit and knew that she was fine. I felt sad I could no longer hug her or talk to her in person, but she felt present to me. She continues to be available to me when I bring her to mind and makes appearances even when I am not thinking about her. Being able to feel her presence in Spirit is comforting. That continues to be the best explanation of why my grieving was different from that of my siblings.

My mother connects through me, or others, frequently. I call on her when I worry about my kids, as I know that she is watching over them. She reassures me that they are okay. She recently came through during a group session held by my coach, with several others participating in person and by phone. My coach has an amazing gift of communicating with those who have transitioned into Spirit as well as angels and other Spirit guides. When it was my turn to receive a message, my mother came through loud and clear. I felt a great healing because Mom told me that she supported me in what I was doing. She wanted me to know of her support even though I may not have felt it when she was alive. Mom wanted me to know that she supported changing my birth name to my spiritual name, Lilia. That was important to me; I had delayed making it my legal name partly out of deference to her. She chose my birth name, after all, and it served me well for most of my life, but my spiritual name resonates with who I am now. It was comforting to know that she approved.

Opening to the Spirit Realm Helps Us Understand the Afterlife

By opening up to our loved ones in the Spirit realm, we can understand better what we will experience when it is our turn to venture into Spirit without our body. Do you know what you are going to face when you leave your body? Do you want to know? We have much information available to us through the stories of those who have had near death experiences (NDEs). Even more is attainable when we communicate with our loved ones and others in Spirit. Each is an individual experience and yet there are commonalities that give me assurance that making the transition into Spirit is not as bad as we may fear. It can feel good because the description of the light and love available to us there is beyond description. The term used most often is "ineffable."

Researchers have identified key elements for those who tell their NDE stories. They include awareness outside the body, intense and generally positive feelings, a tunnel, brilliant or mystical light, encountering other beings, relatives and enlightened ones, life review, and return to the body.[11]

Many of these elements are shared by those who describe life between lives in the regression therapy of Michael Newton[12] and Brian Weiss.[13] It would seem that these characteristics show us what we have to look forward to when we leave our bodies. It does not seem bad: an enhanced awareness, generally positive feelings, and being surrounded by a beautiful, mystical light. There are connections to family and soul group members who have gone on before us. The trials and tribulations of this lifetime are seen without judgment. The mistakes we made are visible to us in a life review, but they seem to be viewed without guilt or shame, just objective observation. This is the kind of information that comes to us from NDE'rs and from those who communicate with people who have passed over. Why not access it through personal communication with those you love and trust or through someone who is gifted in this type of communication?

Receiving messages from loved ones allows us to move from a restrictive grieving process to living a more expansive life, knowing that our loved one is more than fine and watching over us, encouraging us to live life more fully. The more we pay attention to them, the more reassured we are that "death" is not a bad thing.

Connecting to Those in Spirit Helps Them Be of Service

When we connect to loved ones in the Spirit realm, we allow those who have passed over to continue their service.

I once attended a group session with twin psychics who live in my area. Each one in the group received a message or two from those in Spirit. Some were family members. Others were guides who wanted to be helpful by using what they saw from their vantage point and what they learned while living in a body. A medical doctor and an author came through for me. The doctor warned me about challenges to my eyesight. This led me to have an examination that I would not have had and medical advice on what to look out for to avoid a retinal detachment. The author encouraged me to keep writing and assured me that I was on the right track with my book. He continued to serve as an inspiration for me and helped me incorporate more stories into my writing.

The two psychics said many more guides would be coming through with a particular expertise. These guides want to continue the work that they started while on earth. As we open up to their communication, we can allow them to help us. I find this fascinating and know that I have benefitted in small ways. I can see much greater potential as I learn to trust the messages and develop my skills so that I can discern what is helpful and what is not. Love is the key. If the message feels loving, I trust it. If it does not, I ignore it.

When my mother makes an appearance, I know it is because she wants to be helpful. I had to laugh at a message she gave through one of my closest friends who is a gifted intuitive. My friend approached me while I was trying to figure out how to work a projector for a presentation for our nonprofit organization. The person who knew how to set up the machine was not available, so I jumped in to see if I could figure it out. My friend came over to me and said, "I just heard your mother say, 'Susan can do anything.'" (Susan is my birth name.) I burst out laughing, because that was so like Mom. She saw great abilities in me and encouraged me to do whatever I felt like doing. She was the one who suggested that I become a lawyer. She believed in me when I did not. It was encouraging to hear her message come through my friend, and I did figure out how to get the projector working, even though it took a while. I forgot to ask my angels to help. It would have been much easier with their assistance.

Why not allow those who have crossed the veil to continue to serve as we open up to their communications? There are the precautions to take to be sure we are not following flawed guidance, but why not benefit from the wisdom that they gained on earth that is enhanced from the greater perspective they hold in the realm of Spirit?

Connecting to the Spirit Realm Helps Us Serve

We enrich our lives by having the expansive connection to those in Spirit. We can then better serve others here on earth.

As I learn more about what others experience in the Spirit realm, as told by NDE'rs or those who communicate through the veil, I realize that I can bring more of that energy into my life. The love and light described by those who went through what is described as a tunnel of light is so beautiful that witnesses cannot find the words to describe the experience. What if in our meditations and daily practices we intentionally brought in some of that love and light? We can do this as expansively as we can imagine that love and light while understanding that the reality is more than our imagination can hold. It can only uplift and inspire us and help us live in a more loving way.

As we lift ourselves up, we lift others. The more light and love we can bring from beyond the veil into ourselves, the more uplifted we are, and that radiates to those around us.

CHAPTER 7

Communications with Ascended Masters and Other Evolved Spirit Beings

bout a year after I started communicating with Archangel Michael, I was asked to join a group described as a Wisdom Circle. The leader of the group left a successful corporation that he founded so that he could focus on his spiritual gifts. As part of his practice, he brought messages from angels and Ascended Masters. When he started talking about Melchizedek and Saint Germain, I had no idea who he was referring to. I found out later that Melchizedek is mentioned in the Bible. He was the High Priest of Salem, and Jesus was ordained into the Order of Melchizedek. Saint Germain was harder to find information on. (This was before the Internet was so prevalent.) My public library had nothing about him. A friend said she had a book on him and gave it to me. I learned that Saint Germain was known as an Ascended Master. A whole series of books published in the early twentieth century focused on him.

As I developed my skills of communicating with angels, I opened up to messages from Melchizedek and Saint Germain. Later, I opened up to the Egyptian god Thoth and others. They identified themselves by name when I asked, but I inquired only because their energy was distinguishable from Michael's or each other. I would not know how to teach the distinctions to others except to describe it as a different sense of energy.

Since then, I have opened up to the wisdom of other beings called gods and goddesses from Egyptian, Hindu, Celtic, and other cultures. I am amazed by the diversity of beings who are described in sacred texts from around the globe who are communicating through humans more now than ever.

Why develop this kind of communication? It is different than communicating with loved ones across the veil. It is similar to communicating to angels but still different, because most Ascended Masters spent time as human beings. They bring other gifts and a different focus to their messages. We attract to us those who we need most to help us. Melchizedek has different insights and gifts than Saint Germain or Thoth and a different role from that of angels. However, as Ascended Masters, their mastery of life overlaps, so if I ask one something that is the other's expertise, I will not be told, "I don't know. Go ask Thoth." Whatever message needs to get through will get through. I feel that my sense of the Universe is expanded by the multiple entities and their gifts.

When a close friend and I get together to meditate and communicate, we often call in those who come to mind. I can feel the presence of others unnamed, and they add to the loving feeling of that time and place. We settle into the quiet until we sense that one or more wants to speak. It is a sacred practice. I have to feel that the space is safe, that I am connected to my Higher Self, and that I am in alignment with what is good. I appreciate feeling Michael's presence to keep the space safe and protected. It is still scary to speak or write the messages, particularly when someone else is present. When I doubt myself, I ask, *Is that Thoth speaking? Can Metatron really speak through me? Are the Ascended Masters not reserved for experts?*[14]

I have come to know that the right ones for me will come through as appropriate. I need only get my ego out of the way. I don't need to feel small or unworthy, and I don't need to feel special. If you are open to this type of communication and willing to do the work on yourself, I believe you can have similar experiences. It is not for everyone, but if you feel called to it, follow the call, and do what you need to do to allow it happen. Your life will be enriched as mine has. Let your heart lead the way to see if it is for you. If it is, feel honored and blessed, and be willing to do whatever work is needed so that it blesses you and others. Like angels, Ascended Masters are available to help us fulfill our purpose.

One of the sessions with my close friend with whom I love to collaborate was the day before the tenth anniversary of September 11, 2001. There was a lot of fear about what would happen, many conjecturing that some would use that day to create more violence. We used my friend's crystal bowls to help dispel the fear. Crystal bowls have an amazing ability to shift energy and uplift vibration. In that elevated energy, I started speaking a channeled message. It was about envisioning love to dispel fear. After the session, I headed to the ocean, which is two hours from my home. I crossed several bridges over water to get there. Each time I was over a body of water, I sent out messages of love into the water with the intention that it would carry the message to where it was needed. When I got to the beach, I went to the ocean with some friends. I walked to the edge of the water with my arms outstretched, sending waves of love from my heart to the waves crashing on the beach. I saw something splashing in the distance, beyond where people were swimming. The splashes were dolphins jumping and playing in front of me. This was a first for me. I felt that they had heard my message and were letting me know.

My friends and I walked farther down the beach, and I saw some more splashing. I expected to see more dolphins and thought that was great, but these were darker. I saw a fluke instead of a dolphin fin. They were small whales! I felt affirmed in sending out love in the way that I did. It reminded me of a message that James Twyman, the "Peace Troubadour" and founder of the Community of the Beloved Disciple said.[15] He said that if whales and dolphins show up offshore where we can see them, it shows that we are on the right path. Seeing dolphins and whales after sending blessings of love into the waters affirmed that I was on the right path.

This leads me to a story that I told in *Pebbles in the Pond: Transforming the World One Person at a Time, Wave Five*. The chapter is entitled, "The Time Is Now. Are You Ready?" I shared the message that I received from the Egyptian god Thoth.

I had been hearing messages from Thoth for several years. He inspires me to write and gives me guidance for my spiritual work. I have come to respect and trust what I identify as coming from him.

My friend and I were preparing a meditation leading up to the closing ceremony for a group of five-hundred light workers, some of whom had gone to Bolivia with us on that fantastic trip the angels helped me take in 2011. I did not know many of the people in the audience. All were looking forward to the highlight of the three-day conference that was to follow our meditation: a channeling of Metatron through the conference leader, James Tyberonn.[16] As we prepared, we asked what would be most beneficial for this group at the end of three days of inspiration and information. The speakers before us were leading a meditation as part of their presentation. We wanted to do something that complemented their intention but was distinct and designed to prepare for the closing message from Tyberonn.

Before travelling to the conference, we meditated on what we would do with the fifteen minutes given us on the schedule. Our guidance was to bring the wooden staffs that represent the Divine Feminine and Divine Masculine, which we had used in a ceremony before a similar group on December 12, 2012 (12/12/12), a momentous date and occasion. We were asked to wait for additional guidance while we were at the conference. Although we normally plan well ahead of time, we trusted that our allies in Spirit knew better than we did and would help us do exactly what was needed. I was comforted by the fact that we were allotted only a quarter hour, which is easy to fill, particularly as part of a meditation.

On the second day of the conference, we set aside time to receive more guidance on what we were to do. By then we had a sense of the content of the conference and knew what the presenters preceding us were going to do. In the quiet, we asked what would be most helpful. It felt important to talk about the significance of embodying the Divine Feminine and Divine Masculine. The ancient practice of spiritual alchemy asks us to embody both as part of our evolution into higher consciousness. The staffs we brought represented these qualities. My friend's staff represented the Divine Feminine and held the energy of Sekhmet. It felt appropriate that my friend share her story of Sekhmet's message given to her in the Queen's Chamber in the Great Pyramid in Giza.

It was time to ask what I was to share. We knew I was to hold the staff representing the Divine Masculine. We both had experienced the energy of Thoth coming through it. As I quieted my mind, I heard the following.

Tell them this:
Be who you came to be in these bodies.
Do what you came to do in these bodies.
Those in Spirit cannot do what you can do in your bodies.
The time is now.

That was the message I gave before the group of five hundred. I asked myself later, *Did I really stand up in front of five hundred people and deliver a message I said came from the Egyptian god Thoth? Am I crazy?* When standing on the stage before the group, I tuned in and did what I heard my guidance said to say. I felt supported by all of my allies in Spirit. It was scary, but it felt that I was speaking truth, so that is what I delivered.

Not only do I feel that this was an important step along my spiritual path, being who I came to be and doing what I came to do, but I delivered a message that is crucial in these shifting times. We are love. The world needs our love and our light. We share it by discovering our soul's purpose and acting on it.

If you are frightened by the steps required for you to live on purpose, be reassured that you don't need to take a sudden leap into the unknown to be on track. I have taken fifteen or more years to get to where I am at today. You do not have to take the baby steps I have taken. As long as you tune in to your truth, you will find your way. The more you involve your angels and guides, the better an experience you will have. They will connect you to the people who can support you, and they will guide you away from those who slow you down. That is what is so beautiful about developing these connections. Whatever work it requires us to do on ourselves is worth it. The blessings we receive through this process are tenfold or more than what we put into it.

Bringing a beginner's mind to the process helps. Let it be your own process. Let it unfold in your own divine timing. Play with it. Enjoy it. If you do not feel the qualities of joy, peace and love, release whatever is blocking them. If it feels like work, there is something for you to look at. Be compassionate with yourself. Self-judgment will only slow you down. Start the process with asking, and keep going back to that until things start working. Enjoy. That is what they want for you.

More recently, Saint Germain came through in a session I was having with my coach. I had not worked with him in a while, but he showed my coach an amethyst, and she asked me what that meant to me. Saint Germain came to mind, because he is known to use a violet flame for transmutation and transformation, and I associate the violet of an amethyst with his energy. After my session, I conversed with him. He encouraged me not to take lightly what is coming through me. Even when my life's work seems huge, it is important to do whatever necessary to bring it through. He advised me to pay attention to what was happening in connection with time and calendar issues. (I had been double-scheduling myself for the same time slot.) He suggested that I find ways to ground myself. He had me notice how much I enjoyed the experience of my communications with him. It had been a while, and I realized that I feel a deep sense of peace and joy when I connect with him. He asked if I understood why the angels and Ascended Masters had differences in their energy vibration.

I replied, "It has to do with a concept that I heard in church. We are each refracted rays from the source light, and as that refraction we are unique, while at the same time we are one with the source light. The difference is something to do with the angles that the refractions make, and the sacred geometry that is achieved by the angles." [17]

Saint Germain said the following:

You are on the right track. It is more complicated than that and hard to explain in human terminology. It is a good analogy. Without the uniqueness of each refraction, the created world that is the illusion, would not be as it is. Each refraction has a unique frequency or vibration. In that uniqueness there is information, understanding, and wisdom, yet it is only part of the whole. Its essence is the essence of the whole, and yet there is a specificity that helps to contribute to the "created" world in its diversity. Each of us to whom you turn in prayer or sacred communion has a facet of that understanding and wisdom. Collectively, it comes together as the central Truth with a capital "T." From the human perspective, it is so much harder to see the whole. We can help you.

Consider this. If a person prays, their connection to Source—God, the Whole, or All There Is, by whatever name known, said or unsaid—is distorted by their understanding of what that is. They are but a reflection of the whole and yet their essence is the whole. How many humans understand that? Even someone like you who has done so much work does not fully understand. Yogic masters and similar beings who have lifted their human consciousness to a sustained higher vibration glimpse it and live it as well as possible. The great ones like Jesus and Buddha are the exceptions because of the difficulty of doing it. Those of us in Spirit do it more easily. Some of us refined it while in human form. That is why there are the stories of my being able to live so long without aging. That is why there are stories of the miracles performed by other Ascended Masters while they were living and again as they connected to others who opened themselves to their vibrations while still in a body.

Let us return to the focus on you and your mission, your calling, and your book, which will help you fulfill what you came here to do in this body. Are you getting a glimpse? It will require you to lift your vibration higher than you have before and to hold that vibration in your body so that others can experience it and be inspired by it. This is not the work of a novice, but you are not a novice and you know it! I should say that you have allowed yourself to know it at times and then reject it, but you keep working on yourself, because deep down you know the truth.

There are many more like you who have heard the call and are not sure how to answer it. Those are the ones that you are writing to. It is time to awaken. This is a turning point in America's history. The world is starving and thirsting for real love. Help them to awaken to it inside themselves. Their divine spark has not gone out, but for the majority, it is quite dim. Fan the flames with light and love, with hope, with awareness, with understanding. We in Spirit are here to help, but as Thoth said, we cannot do what you can do in human bodies. It is in the dimension of 3-D on earth, in human bodies, that the vibrations of a shift in consciousness can shift the vibrations in the rest of creation. What you have miscreated needs to be transmuted while you are in human bodies.

Ah! That triggered a memory, did it not? Now you know why I mentioned amethyst as the trigger to connect to me. It was for you to remember all that you learned about the violet flame and the transmutation process. You forgot about that, didn't you? You used to use it on a regular basis, but not recently.

The importance of doing this while in body is that the vibration in cellular memory is heightened and begins to entrain others, affecting your DNA and the DNA on the planet. This cannot be done through spiritual energy. It requires material energy vibrating at those higher levels. That is how the shift occurs. Matter to matter. It is true that the material world is an illusion, but it is more about your perception of the material world that is the illusion. Matter is dense energy. Do you know what it takes to have energy condense to that density and have life forms develop from that? What if more people contemplated the origins of life rather than arguing over who is right? Whatever theory is used, whether it is Creationists who

interpret the Bible literally or those on the other end of
the spectrum, what is important is that in reflecting on
the question, one can have a sense of awe at whatever
answer is given.

*Life in a body is precious, but it is not all there is.
Life goes on beyond the body. The wondrous knowing
that life goes on after death should not diminish the
miracle of life on earth.*

*Your mission, Ms. Rae of light, is to help humans
understand and appreciate the miracle of being human
and to know that as awesome a miracle as life in a
body is, the miraculous nature of life itself, life as
consciousness life as Spirit, is so much greater that
humans can access only a glimmer of it. You know the
expression "beyond the beyond"? Truth is that which is
incomprehensible by the human brain, and yet humans
can understand that Truth is what makes life in a body
so holy and precious.*

*Once people have a glimmer of Truth with a capital
"T," they will glimpse the love, joy, and peace that
accompany it. Once they get it, they can love each other
even if their personal truth resides on the opposite side
of the spectrum.*

*Your task is to help people connect to that spark of
divinity within. It can be fanned by the wings of angels
into a glowing flame that radiates into the world and
warms the life of the next person. In that warmth, the*

other person can be inspired to connect to their inner spark and find a way for it to glow. This is easily done by asking angels to fan the flame.

One candle to candle, one heart to heart. It does not take much.

I realize that this is a lengthy message, but it felt so important that I shared all of it. It gives a sense of the different type of message that Saint Germain is likely to bring, compared to Michael. There is more humor and playfulness along with the deep meaning of his message.

I want to note that there are common themes in the messages that come through me. My understanding is that the messages are coming through my filter, so they use what I know as a human. They know what concepts have particular resonance for me. As an example, the idea of "truth with a capital 'T' " is something I focus on in my learning discernment practices and when using consensus for group decisions. I know that I can get only a glimpse of the Divine Truth that merits a capital "T." My personal truth aligns with Divine Truth as I use discernment practices and remove bias or distortion based on conditioning, but I realize that it is impossible to know absolute Divine Truth. Several of the angel's messages refer to this concept because they know I understand the underlying meaning.

Another theme is that each of us has a divine spark that can be fanned into a glowing flame. I first heard this from a spiritual teacher in human form. The angels and Ascended Masters frequently refer to it, because it describes enlightenment in terms that make sense to me. It provides an image that I can understand with my mind and my heart. I can see and feel greater light as I intentionally fan the flame of my divine spark and ask the angels to help me do so.

As you develop your communication with angels and Ascended Masters, you are likely to see some common themes. With further practice, the messages will become more universal. They will hold truth that feels even more aligned with truth with a capital "T." It is all a process. Open to it, and allow it to transform you.

CHAPTER 8

Fairies and Other Elementals

As I was writing this book, I attended a class for developing intuitive abilities. Even though I have intuitive gifts that have opened me up to the Spirit realm, I know that I can become even more skilled through learning other techniques.

At the end of the classes, the teacher had us do an intuitive reading for someone in the group. She made it fun so that we did not stress about it. Worry or anxiousness about getting a correct and relevant message does not enhance intuitive abilities.

One night, the woman reading for me said that she saw a beautiful being in a white, flowing gown. Its wings were iridescent green and blue. The woman was not sure who or what the being was, but she said the being wanted me to know that it would help me finish my book.

The next morning I went into meditation to connect with this being. She let me know she was a fairy, not an angel. She asked me to share some of my experiences with fairies in the book, because they too want to help humans.

I knew little about communicating with fairies. I knew they were part of the elementals, along with elves, leprechauns, water sprites, and others that most people believe belong only in storybooks. My limited experience came from sessions I had with healers and through reading Doreen Virtue's book *Healing with the Fairies.*[18]

My first experience with them was when I went to a shamanic healer. I had limited experience with shamanic healings, but this woman was highly recommended, so I signed up for a session with her. I did not know what to expect but was open to any opportunity to work on myself to become a clearer conduit of love and light.

Shamanic journeys can differ greatly, but the intent is to have an experience in the spiritual realm that will lead to physical, emotional, or spiritual healing. Different schools of shamanism have different rituals but many include a ritual in which the healer or client or both visualize a journey that provides information or an experience that heals.

She took me on a journey unlike any I had experienced before. We ended up going to dimensions where fairies live energetically. The healer told me what she saw, and

I could visualize it as she shared. I was greeted as if they knew me, and they welcomed me back. This was curious because as far as I knew, I had no conscious interactions with fairies.

During this session, the lead fairy, the Fairy Queen, asked me to lie on the ground. She said they wanted to do surgery to heal my broken heart. They cut open my heart (in my imagination and the healer's visualization). They stitched together the parts that had been ripped open by my heartbreaks and then the fairies sewed up my heart. (I had not shared with the healer my history of broken hearts, so it was quite interesting that this was the focus of the healing.) They asked me to keep a statue of a fairy around so that I would remember the experience and allow my heart to fully heal.

At the end of the session the healer commented that it was an unusual journey, but it was what had shown up for her. I am still not sure what to make of it, but it seemed like a real occurrence, albeit in another dimension.

I had one other session in which fairies came to work with me. It was with a friend who has amazing intuitive abilities and is able to give verbal messages from many types of beings in the Spirit realm. (I am blessed to have so many friends with astounding intuitive and healing gifts.) In this session, which was several years after the shamanic session, a Fairy Queen came and told me that I would do well to open up to my fairy energy. Again, this seemed odd, and yet other messages through this friend had always resonated and seemed to hold truth for me.

With these experiences, I decided to explore fairies by reading Doreen Virtue's book, *Healing With the Fairies*. As I understood it, communication with fairies can be done in the same way as with angels, but fairies have a different energy and purpose. Doreen tells how fairies helped to heal her and how they want to work with humans to make Earth a better place to live. If you are interested in communicating with fairies, read her book.

Why am I writing about fairies if I have had only a few mysterious encounters with them? I know they exist, even if I have not opened up fully to their energy. They want to get my attention, or they would not have spoken to my classmate that night. I believe that they want to help us like angels do, though they have a different role, because they are so connected to earth energy. Some will want to develop a relationship with them, while others will not.

Using the AOLTA method will work for fairies. Who knows what gifts of healing and encouragement they can bring if you open up to them?

I opened up to the one who said she would help me complete this book, and the following is our conversation.

Do you have a name?

My name is Elena. There are others who would love to converse with you, but I was the bolder one who stepped forward the other night.

Can I ask why you want to talk to me and help me with this book?

Humans need to be encouraged to communicate with us as well as the angels. Each of the elementals has a separate purpose and way to assist life on Earth. Your soul has chosen a purpose of bringing heaven to earth even though heaven exists here from our perspective. It is humans who have so much trouble seeing it and living it. If you would open up to our energy, you would know it more fully. We would help you feel joy and laughter and all the good things of life—not the suffering and sorrow most of you wallow in.

We know that you are writing this book to help more people open up to angels. You even have your chapters on communicating with loved ones and Ascended Masters, but you left us out, and so I spoke up. I wanted to help you complete your book by adding us to the mix.

You know I don't have much experience with fairies. I have friends who know a lot more than I do. Why ask me to write about you?

Your readers will want to open up to Spirit in any way that they can. They are ready but not sure about how to do it. I know there are other books, but your book is going to reach other readers, and we wanted them to know that your process works for us as well. Look around you. Don't you think the world would be a better place if more people knew fairies existed and opened up to their energy?

I do. I know that my life would be enhanced if I opened up more. I know that when I am aware of the possibility of your existence, I am more careful where I walk and how. I know that the messages that came through Doreen Virtue's book encouraged greater environmental sensitivity and appreciation for the elemental energies that support creation on this planet. I don't question the value of more people acquainting themselves with fairy energy, but I was surprised that one of you would contact me through another person and ask to be included in this book when I have so little expertise.

I would like to ask another question. In my two healing sessions, I was described as having a life as a fairy. I have had friends who say I have fairy energy, but I also relate to being an earth angel. How does that work? Can humans have lived lives as fairies, and can humans embody both fairy and angel energy?

You may want to ask your angel friends for a more comprehensive answer. There are many humans who embody fairy energy and who have had lives as fairies. You know that a soul can incarnate in many ways. They can even incarnate in other parts of the Universe or farther realms of creation. The possibilities of life in form are endless, because the possibilities for creation are endless. If you check inside your heart, you will know that you have had many types of lives, and you have brought much of that energy into this life. It has been confusing, because you chose to live in middle America with middle-class values and middle-of-the-road politics. That does not allow for much exploration into the worlds you have travelled before, yet you managed to open up some doors. We decided to help you open up some more. (Felt smile.)

Thank you, Elena. I appreciate this information and your persistence to get through to me, even if through someone else. That must be one of the reasons I felt so compelled to attend the intuitive development class.

We were glad to see you there. We were hoping there would be an opening through one of your classmates, and there was. You followed it up with your research and your writing. We thank you for that.

Elena, if it is okay with you, I would now like to address Michael with respect to the rest of the questions I asked.

Michael, dearest beloved Michael. You have been so patient with me over the years and you have watched me open up, close down, and open again. Now there is new information that I am being asked to open up to. What advice can you give me or anyone else who feels connected to both angel and fairy energy?

It is all Spirit, different forms with different intentions and roles. Just like you often talk about how you prefer variety in your ice cream and pizza, not to mention your diverse methods of meditation. You like to sample all sorts of different experiences. So have you done in terms of sampling life. You have angel energy. You have fairy energy. What is important is that in this lifetime, in this body, you bring through as much love and light as you can and inspire and teach others to do the same. The love and light that you ground into the Earth's atmosphere will help the planet and all its inhabitants, elementals included. Those who are not in body cannot do what you can do in a body. That was a key part of the message that came through you from Thoth. It is a major concept that we hope you will bring through your work. Start with your own practices, and encourage others to do the same. You will see the impact in your life and the lives around you. You already do. You know that your work life and family life is much better than many others experience. A huge part of it is the love and light you have consciously chosen to embody. It has been a major part of your practice even if you were not always aware. The energy work will help, because it will help people clear the energy blocks and allow more light and love to flow. It is not something done in the imagination. It has a physical and emotional impact. The more you visualize and set specific intentions around it, the more it will be so.

Thank you, Michael. This is a lot to absorb, but I feel that this is important. Thank you so much.

Since receiving these messages, I have been touching in to both the fairy energy and the angel energy that feels as if it is in my body. This is a work in progress, but I already feel able to access a sense of greater love and light. I realize that love and light are more complex than my brain can comprehend, yet like the concept of truth with a capital "T," I have a sense of understanding that aligns with a much greater meaning.

I invite you to explore the fairy realm if you feel drawn to it. See what insight you receive from the elemental dimension. Observe whether contacts with fairies increase your quotient for love and light in your body. You may find yourself smiling more and skipping here and there in the delight of more expanded living. Maybe they will remind you that heaven is here on earth. Ask them to open your life to more of it, and see what happens.

PART III

BASIC TRUTHS THAT ANGELS AND ASCENDED MASTERS HAVE TAUGHT ME

O ver the years, the angels and Ascended Masters have taught me key principles for living in a soul-inspired manner. Each principle is simple and basic, yet elusive in comprehending and accomplishing it. Because they have meant so much in my spiritual practice and inquiry, I include them here.

CHAPTER 9

Know Thyself

The phrase "Know Thyself" is engraved over the Temple of Apollo at Delphi in Greece. It is included in many books on spiritual development as a requirement for self-realization. It relates to a question we all ask ourselves at some point: "Who am I?" We answer it superficially through what we identify with: our role in family life, our job, and our passions. Part of knowing ourselves is recognizing who we are not: our personality, ego, and the other mental or emotional structures that are part of human nature. It involves understanding the concept of being spiritual beings in a human body as most great teachers tell us. We can know that we are more than our personality. We can believe that we have a soul and may connect to our essence, but do we know who we are? Yogi masters and other spiritual teachers ask their students this question. It leads to a process of discovery more than an actual answer.

A tool that I have used for personal discovery since 1989 is the Enneagram.[19] It allowed me to see how unhealthy my marriage was and how ingrained the patterns were. I knew that I needed to get out of the marriage to be able to work on myself. I was smart enough to know that I could not change my husband, yet I could not stay married without significant change in his behavior. By seeing our personality dynamics as indicated by the Enneagram, I saw that the best thing for me was to sever ties and do my work apart from him.

Many other practices and tools exist to help us discover our real identity: meditation and contemplation, yogic practices, shamanic practices, and many more. Just being willing to ask ourselves "Who am I?" moves us to a greater understanding. Asking our angels, Ascended Masters, and spiritual guides to help us with this inquiry enhances whatever we do on our own. Having a spiritual mentor or teacher to show us our blind spots helps. As I go deeper with this question, I recognize how much more there is to the answer. I am grateful that the angels and other spiritual guides have made it clear that it is a vital question for our life as spiritual beings in a human body.

CHAPTER 10

Love Yourself

Do you love yourself? If you knew yourself, you would. In the meantime, you can ask the angelic realm to help you with this practice, because they are more adept at being love, sharing love, and showing you the love you are. Michael has told me I am loved and I am love many times! I can sense it when he tells me and open up to it in the moment. I see myself through a lens of criticism, judgment, shame, guilt, or the perception of the moment. My ego does not want to accept the love that I am. Perhaps my ego feels like it will evaporate or disintegrate if I embody and embrace the love that I am.

It feels right to ask Michael in this moment to say what he has observed in me and in others. Here is his response.

Lilia, I have seen you fully embrace yourself many times as the love you are. Through doing work on yourself and going deep into meditation, you have experienced the bliss and ecstasy that is possible when one opens up to the truth of who they are—love in human form. Most of your life is spent in a much less joyful state, as you well know. Sometimes you had great trouble even believing that you could feel that love for yourself again. I remind you often, and sometimes you believe me. Most of the time you appreciate it, yet you don't feel it. This is true of most in human form. It is a part of the human consciousness that you and other light workers are helping to heal as you heal the disconnect and disbelief in yourself. Know that your healing and your evolution is not just for you. It is also for others. That is what the sayings "as above, so below; as below, so above; as within, so without" are about.

If humans could open up to the love they are and truly love themselves—even for short periods—the shift on earth would be palpable. Those of us in the angelic realm are reflecting this love back to you. We see the love you are and reflect it back. It often bounces off your hard exteriors, your hardened hearts, your prison-like defenses, built by the personality but shielding you from both harm and good. Love is a protective force. If you allow yourselves to be that love, you would not feel the need to put up these artificial barriers that keep you from loving yourself and others.

Thank you, Michael.

CHAPTER 11

Be Here Now

Be Here Now by Ram Dass was published in the 1970s.[20] I remember reading it and thinking, *This is all we need to do. Live in the present moment. Bring our presence to the present.* I am still learning how to do that. It is one of the hardest things to do in spite of being inspired by gurus like Ram Dass and others who understand this concept as crucial for spiritual development.

For me, it involves bringing my attention to the present moment and having "presence" in the now. Bringing my attention to the present means recognizing when my mind is focused on the past or future, and it is consciously bringing awareness to the moment. We spend most of our time oblivious to whether we are living in the past, present, or future. Most of us do not realize we are unaware, since we move through life on autopilot. Our heads are often spinning around in circles, trying to figure out how to solve a problem or worrying about a future issue. No wonder we go around searching for solutions. The answer is in the now, not in the future.

We spend a lot of time feeling shame, blame, grief, frustration, and other emotions that keep us mired in the past. Whatever is done is done. "The moving finger having writ, moves on," the wise Omar Khayyam said. Anything to be learned or healed from past experience must be done in the moment. We have to bring our awareness to the present to do so.

Presence in the now involves awareness of the body, mind, and heart. We have a tendency to be in one or two but rarely all three. Full presence in the present moment requires alignment of body, mind, and heart and then connecting to our soul and to Spirit. This is not an easy task because of our habitual nature and automatic preference for one type of attention over another.

Angels help us in this. To communicate with them, we need to quiet our thoughts and align our heart, body, and mind. That is how we open up and listen to them. Otherwise, the communications become garbled. The preparation steps they recommend for us to listen to them are described in chapter 3.

All is created from the eternal now, but we keep forgetting to connect to it as we try to manifest in life. I know that I do. It takes conscious choice and discipline to return the awareness to the present, fully aligned in mind, body, and heart. Doing that, we can connect to our souls and to the rest of the Spirit realm, including the blessed angels, who are doing their best to help us.

CHAPTER 12

As Above, So Below; As Below, So Above; As Within, So Without

If you have spent much time in spiritual circles, you have probably heard of the mythic and mystical Emerald Tablets. Because Thoth has had a huge impact in my life, I feel that he made sure I heard about them and explored their meaning. He is believed to have written the Emerald Tablets used by the Pharaoh Akhenaten in Egypt and found by Alexander the Great in 332 BCE.[21] Most students of sacred mysteries believe that the Emerald Tablets existed and contained the concepts "as above, so below; as below, so above." Some add the idea of "as within, so without." Because the Emerald Tablets held great wisdom that threatened those in power, many versions of them were destroyed. At least one source survived in Arabic through the writings of the Turkish mystic Balinas.[22]

Like the principles in this chapter there is a simplicity to these phrases, and yet it is almost impossible to fully understand them. It is a process of inquiry that shapes you as you inquire further and realize how little you know. It is an amazing process whereby the more you learn, the less knowledgeable you feel.

As Michael alluded to, what we do and how we do it impacts more people than just ourselves. We do not live in isolation, even if we live as a recluse. This concept is connected to our living as spiritual beings in a human body. How we live our human lives affects our soul and those connected to our soul, which in some theories means all of the rest of existence.

I asked Michael to explain this better. This is his reply.

Consider yourself as the point at the middle of a circle. This has long been a symbol for the sun and the god Ra. Consider further that the circle is infinitely large, for that is what the rest of existence is. That idea is difficult to hold in the mind and impossible to draw on paper, yet that is the truth of life. Each being is at the center of an infinite Universe and the experience of the self impacts the rest of all there is. As above, so below;

*as below, so above; as within, so without. This relates to
the concept of oneness.*

Thank you, Michael. I have contemplated the
symbol of Ra and used it as the symbol for the sun
in astrology. In sacred geometry, we can start with
a point and bring in a second point to draw a line
segment. If we have that second point travel around
the first while keeping the length of the line segment
the same, the result is a circle, which is the symbol
for the sun. A circle can be drawn around the second
point using the first point, and the intersection of
the two circles forms a vesica piscis, considered by
many scholars of sacred geometry to be the womb
of creation. Repeating this many times results in a
seed of life, a flower of life, ad infinitum. I feel like
this sacred symbolism of circles relates to what you
just said.

*Yes, although it is hard to extrapolate, because
each circle you are describing is finite. The flower of life
represents the connectedness in life. As you know, these
circles can be connected with lines, and the result can
be shown to be the metatronic cube and platonic solids,
considered to be the building blocks of life. The lines
are considered masculine, while the circles represent
the feminine nature of creation. You have studied and*

taught all of this in your sacred geometry classes. The mystery represented by these symbols is that while each intersection is a point, each point is infinitesimally small. It has no size, and yet it has a location in reference to all of the other points. From one point, all the other points expand into infinity. There is no limit to the number of additional points created as the flower of life pattern is extended. It shows the representation of life from infinitely small to infinitely large, in the same way that the single circle does, although with less simplicity. Neither symbolic representation helps a student who sees the black and white and not beyond or who does not engage with the symbol to find meaning.

What is most important about these contemplations is that one is seeking some understanding of truth. If one understands that what they do and how they are being has impact well beyond themselves, it can motivate them to live with as much love as possible, so that becomes the force of impact on others.

Thank you, Michael.

It amazes me how profound the contemplation of a circle or other sacred shapes can be. Even the concepts of the Emerald Tablets have such depth and universal application that despite their simplicity, they lead to greater understanding of the web of life.

CHAPTER 13

We Are One

Afinal principle that evades comprehension is that we are one, and yet unique. We are one with all creation and yet we have no way of knowing the extent of all creation. We can only have a sense of how much we do not know. We realize that through our limited brain capacities, senses, and other human abilities we cannot know the extent of our physical creation, let alone what exists in other dimensions. We cannot know how many other dimensions there are. We may receive guidance from the angelic realm, and yet we cannot know how much more there is beyond that. Words are limitations in understanding as shown consistently by those who have NDEs and struggle to describe the "ineffable." We have to create words for inexplicable concepts.

I asked Michael to expand on these comments. This is what he said.

The earlier concepts are related. This one is focused on the fabric of life being love. When a person recognizes that all of creation is love, they may understand that God is love. As you have learned in the Unity tradition, there is no place that God is not, so all of life is love even if it does not act loving. It is a hard concept for the human brain to embrace. Full understanding is not required, because just as the last one can inspire a person to act with love, so can the concept of oneness. Even without grasping the meaning of oneness, humans can have the sense that love is the creative force in life. Aligning more with love can improve their life and open them up to the possibility of it improving the lives of others.

Thank you again, Michael. It has been wonderful to have your help in explaining these concepts. The ideals are beyond third-dimensional knowing, but they have a way of helping us align with what feels true and good. In that same manner, angels have a way of helping us align to what feels true and good.

I am grateful for your loving support, even when I ignored your guidance and allowed my humanness to block the true and good that you have brought through to me. Time and time again you have been there for me, reminding me that I am loved and that I am love.

Conclusion

My wish is that you use the examples of my foibles and fumblings, as well my successes and lessons learned, to bring more joy, peace, and love into your life as you practice the art of listening to angels and other beings of light and love. I hope you will see from my stories that you do not have to be perfect to be on this path. You can be imperfect and slow to learn, and angels will still love you and be there to guide you as you take each step and ask for their help.

I feel honored and privileged to step into the role of a messenger for these radiant, loving messengers of the Divine. May your life be blessed and enriched as you practice this art.

Ashe. And so it is.[23]

About the Author

After thirty years as a state legislative lawyer, Lilia Shoshanna Rae decided she could no longer postpone her passion as a messenger for the angelic realm to help create heaven on earth. She shares her story of how angels entered her life and helped her transform it by opening to their wisdom and love. She shares the five-step process they gave her to develop the art of listening to angels.

After angels began communicating with Lilia, she developed her skills as a Reiki master and a teacher of the sacred mysteries of alchemy, sacred geometry, and the Enneagram. Lilia also has a unique talent for leading meditations to help clients attain deep states of peace and access inner wisdom. With angelic guidance, she developed the "Stellar Healing" protocol in which she accesses star energy to give clients an expanded awareness and new perspective on issues in their lives.

Lilia is a contributing author in two editions of *Pebbles in the Pond: Transforming the World One Person at a Time*. In her chapter in *Wave One,* "Life Is a Hoot If We'd Only Laugh," she gives the reader three tools for continuing their transformational practice, including the gift of laughter. Her chapter in *Wave Five,* "The Time Is Now. Are You Ready?" shares guidance for all of us to be who we came here to be and do what we came here to do.

Lilia also blogs on topics of practical mysticism, angels, and the transforming power of the Enneagram. Her writing is found at LiliaShoshannaRae.com/blog.

NOTES

1 Trudy Griswold and Barbara Mack, *Angelspeake: How to Talk with Your Angels* (New York: Simon & Schuster, 1995).

2 G. W. Hardin and Julia Ingram, *The Messengers: A True Story of Angelic Presence and the Return to the Age of Miracles* (New York: Pocket Books, 1996).

3 Sinda Jordan, *Inspired by Angels: Letters from the Archangels Michael, Raphael, Gabriel, and Uriel* (Nevada City, CA: Blue Dolphin Publishing, 1998).

4 Kimberly Marooney, *The Angel Blessings Kit: Cards of Sacred Guidance and Inspiration* (Beverly, MA: Fair Winds Press, 1995).

5 Marooney, *Angel Blessings Kit*, 36.

6 Marooney, *Angel Blessings Kit*, 72.

7 *A Course in Miracles* (Viking: Foundation for Inner Peace, 1996).

8 Luke 17:21 (New International Version).

9 Diana Cooper, *A Little Light on Angels* (The Park, Findhorn: Findhorn Press, 1996).

10 Caroline Myss, *Sacred Contracts* (New York: Harmony Books, 2001).

11 *See, e.g.* Elisabeth Kubler-Ross, MD, *The Tunnel and the Light: Essential Insights on Living and Dying* (New York: Marlow & Co, 1999); Raymond A. Moody, Jr., MD, *Life after Life* (New York: Harper Collins, 1975); Jeffrey Long, MD, with Paul Perry, *Evidence of the Afterlife: The Science of Near-Death Experiences* (New York: Harper Collins, 2010).

12 Michael Newton, *Destiny of Souls: New Case Studies of Life between Lives* (St. Paul, MN: Llewellyn Publications, 2000).

[13] Brian L. Weiss, MD, *Many Lives, Many Masters* (New York: Simon & Schuster, 1988).

[14] James Tyberonn is a well-known and respected channeler of Metatron as well as one of my mentors and friends. He is the author of several books including *Earth-Keeper Chronicles: Metatron Speaks*. Earth-keeper.com.

[15] I participated in James Twyman's Community of the Beloved Disciple in the late 1990s when he talked about the signs we received from dolphins and whales (www.JamesTwyman.com).

[16] James Tyberonn is the facilitator of Earth-Keeper conferences and pilgrimages as well as a channeler and author.

[17] Dale Allen Hoffman is an Aramaic scholar. He presented this concept on vibrations of souls at a workshop held close to my home(www.DaleAllenHoffman.com).

[18] Doreen Virtue, *Healing with the Fairies* (Carlsbad, CA: Hay House, 2001).

[19] The Enneagram is a study of the dynamics of personality development and spiritual evolution based on a diagram with nine points along a circle. First taught in mystery schools from teacher to student, it is a valuable tool for self-discovery. See www.enneagraminstitute.com for excellent information on the subject.

[20] Ram Dass, *Be Here Now* (New Mexico: Lama Foundation, 1971).

[21] Christine Page, MD, *2012 and the Galactic Center* (Rochester, VT: Bear Company, 2008), 189–192.

[22] Christine Page, MD, *2012 and the Galactic Center* (Rochester, VT: Bear Company, 2008), 192.

[23] *Ashe* is an African word that means "And so it is." I have been using it in my spiritual practice because it seems to have a different vibration, and it feels appropriate to use it here.

43279439R00099

Made in the USA
Middletown, DE
05 May 2017